S0-BAI-035

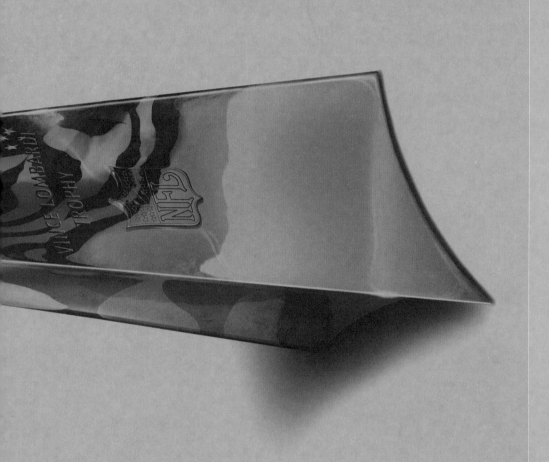

AFC-NFC World Championship Game
Sunday, February 3, 2002·5:00 P.M.
Louisiana Superdome, New Orleans

$400 ALL TAXES INCLUDED
GATES OPEN AT 1:00 P.M.

PATRIOTS UNITED

THE NEW ENGLAND PATRIOTS
WORLD CHAMPIONSHIP SEASON

PATRIOTS UNITED

THE NEW ENGLAND PATRIOTS WORLD CHAMPIONSHIP SEASON

BY BRYAN MORRY

EDITED BY FRED KIRSCH AND CHRYS GOYENS

     TEAM POWER PUBLISHING INC.   TRÉCARRÉ @ QUEBECOR MEDIA

TABLE OF CONTENTS

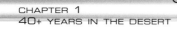

CATALOGUING IN PUBLICATION DATA

Morry, Bryan, 1971-

Patriots United: The New England Patriots World Championship Season
Written by Bryan Morry   Edited by Chrys Goyens and Fred Kirsch

1. New England Patriots (Football team)   2. Super Bowl (36th: 2002: New Orleans, LA)
I. Goyens, Chrys, 1949-   II. Kirsch, Fred, 1961-   III. Title

GV956.N48M67 2002   796.332'64'09744   C2002-903497-3   ISBN 2-89568-076-0

Legal deposit, second quarter, 2002   National Library of Canada   Bibliothèque nationale du Québec

COPYRIGHT ©2002
ALL RIGHTS RESERVED BY NEW ENGLAND PATRIOTS, LP
One Patriot Place, Foxborough, MA 02035 USA

No part of this book may be reproduced or transmitted in any form or by any means
electronic, chemical or mechanical, including photocopying, nor held in any information
storage or retrieval system without permission in writing from the New England Patriots.

PRINTED AND BOUND IN CANADA BY
QUEBECOR WORLD INC. IN AUGUST 2002

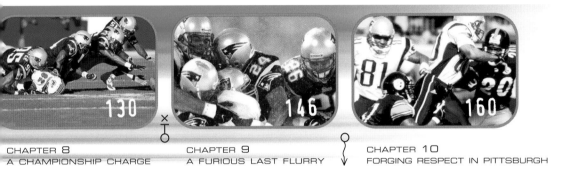

A FEW MUSINGS ON A MIRACLE IN THE BIG EASY

The feeling is still there. No, not the same lightning bolt surge that shot through me when Adam Vinatieri started dancing with this kick just about halfway to greatness. At 66 years of age there was no way I thought I could ever feel 18 again. But that's the way it was, when after following the Patriots from Day One as the official scorer of their very first game on September 9, 1960 (a loss to the lowly Denver Broncos), it finally happened. The Patriots won the Super Bowl for the first time and could say they were the best team in football. About an hour later, walking through the press box in a still electric Louisiana Superdome, I was face to face with "The Duke," Gino Cappelletti.

Gino and I were there at the beginning of the franchise, and still have regular contact with the team. The Duke is part of their radio team. I'm a sportswriter. I said, "Now we're one for 42." The reply was a big smile from Cappelletti, who offered, "It was worth the wait."

At least twice a week when I first awake and gather my thoughts for the day, it hits me. The Patriots won the Super Bowl. Frankly, I know it happened, but I still have a hard time believing it. I mentioned this psychological ambivalence to Jeff Lurie, owner of the Philadelphia Eagles. Jeff grew up in Brookline, Mass., a Patriots fanatic, and tried to buy the team but was outbid by Bob Kraft. When I told him about my recurring wake-up call, he laughed: "You? ... It happens to me three times a week. It's the most incredible thing I've seen in sports."

I sat with Bill Parcells and former Green Bay Packer general manager Ron Wolf, waiting out a rain delay at an exhibition baseball game in Florida.

I asked them, two of the most successful people in the National Football League the previous two decades, "Where does the Patriots victory rank in Super Bowl history?"

Parcells was first to respond. "From start to finish, it's the best coaching job anyone has done."

Wolf was equally succinct. "It's the greatest victory of any Super Bowl team. Number one. They won it all with a waiver wire team."

To New England's fans, and many others across the nation, this is what made the Patriots victory so special. It was so unexpected. The team was likeable. It met difficult challenges and defeated them.

This is a team that could finish, either by driving for the winning score, or by stopping the other team from overtaking it at the end. It didn't throw away a game in the fourth quarter, which had been a hallmark of so many Patriot teams in the past, even the good ones.

In March, I bumped into Broncos head coach Mike Shanahan, one of the few coaches in the league who gave the Patriots a chance when I spoke to him before the playoffs began. Before I could say a word, Shanahan offered: "What other team has been 24th on defense, 19th on offense, and number one at the end? I bet there has never been another team like that."

He's right. I checked with the NFL and they said the only team even remotely close to those numbers was the 1980 Oakland Raiders, one of the rare wild card teams to go all the way to win the Super Bowl. The Raiders were 16th and 11th... far beyond 24th and 19th. In contrast, the heavily favored St. Louis Rams lined up for their climactic game with the Patriots at first on offense and third on defense.

Despite the numbers, their coach, Mike Martz, architect of the so-called "Greatest Show on Turf," knew Super Bowl XXXVI was going to be a battle to the finish.

"When we beat them up in New England during the season, I told our team not to be surprised if we had to play them again in the Super Bowl. They knocked six of our players out of the game that night, and no one had done that to our team. I told the press after the game they were the best team we had played all year, and I meant it. Of all the teams I have watched over the years in pro football, the quality they had that no other team had, was that all three areas of the game – offense, defense, special teams – were played at a high level of intensity. There was no drop-off and they carried this through the entire game."

Former Patriots coach Dick MacPherson called the season "a miracle," and in retrospect, it certainly was. Super Bowl winning teams seldom if ever had to deal with a lot of adversity during the season.

The Patriots overcame the death of respected quarterbacks coach Dick Rehbein, a life-threatening injury to team star Drew Bledsoe, a series of injuries to their linebackers that altered their defensive scheme, a 1-3 start, the ridiculous maneuverings of Terry Glenn, and three solid teams in the playoffs – Oakland, Pittsburgh and St. Louis – to win it all.

"They are a team that found a way to win," said Steelers coach Bill Cowher. "Each game it was a little different. In our game, they beat us on two special-team plays. A punt return for a touchdown (Troy Brown) and a blocked field goal for a touchdown. Other than that, they didn't do much, but they did what they had to do to win, and we didn't."

And at the end, their closer was ready. Adam Vinatieri delivered the biggest kick in team history for the 20-17 victory, and an emotional boost that might have been the greatest in the history of New England. Vinatieri had never missed a kick in a domed stadium, and was six-for-six in overtime in his career. So even though it was shocking emotionally, statistically it was no surprise that his winning field goal went straight between the posts, providing a link to start and finish. The first three points in Patriots history came from the foot of Cappelletti; the last of the championship season from Vinatieri.

"This victory made everyone who was ever a Patriots player, or a Patriots fan, feel proud to be a Patriots fan," said Cappelletti. "This is the first season ever when it all finished right. It was clean."

Will McDonough

Will McDonough

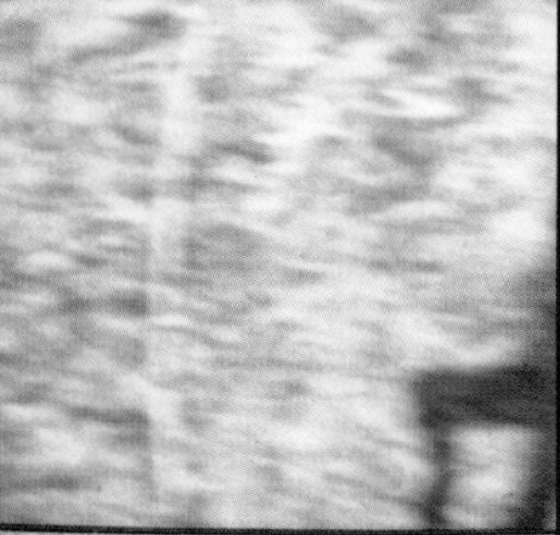

CHAPTER 1

40+ YEARS
IN THE DESERT

THE FOOTBALL ARCED HIGH AND TRUE,

SPLITTING THE UPRIGHTS DEAD CENTER

AND SENDING NEW ENGLAND INTO

PAROXYSMS OF DELIGHT. THE MIRACLE

HAD FINALLY HAPPENED TO A FRANCHISE

IN MIDDLE AGE. THE DATE, FEBRUARY 3,

2002, WOULD HENCEFORTH RESIDE

IN GLORY, THE MOST FAMOUS DATE

IN PATRIOTS HISTORY.

JIM LEE HUNT AND LARRY EISENHAUER DISLODGE THE FOOTBALL FROM FALCONS QUARTERBACK RANDY JOHNSON

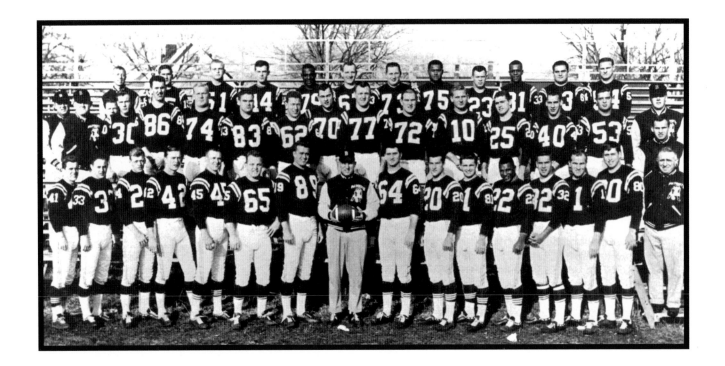

The other significant date in the Patriots story is November 22, 1959, the day William H. "Billy" Sullivan committed his meager resources to establish the Boston Patriots of the upstart American Football League. His venture was the fifth of its kind in the region – the Boston Bulldogs, Boston Braves/Redskins, Boston Yanks and Providence Steam Roller had represented the region as local professional football franchises over the decades. None had lasted and it was a popular belief that Boston was not fertile territory for the pro game.

The daring Irishman was the epitome of style over substance; no rich man's son or carpetbagger he. Sullivan, (Boston College, Class of '37) spent time working at his alma mater upon graduation before moving on to Notre Dame, the United States Naval Academy and the National League's Boston Braves as director of public relations. In 1955, he left sports to work for the Metropolitan Petroleum Company and three years later, was the firm's president – the title he held as he diligently labored to bring professional football to New England's hub.

Unlike most professional sports team owners, Sullivan was not obscenely wealthy and scraped together the necessary funds alongside a consortium of investors to solidify the eighth and final AFL franchise that would battle the established National Football League for supremacy. In New England, that meant convincing local New York Giants fans to embrace their new home team – no easy task without immediate on-field success. His Boston Patriots, homeless throughout their first decade, persevered through a lean inaugural season before establishing themselves as an AFL contender.

ABOVE THE INAUGURAL NEW ENGLAND PATRIOTS SQUAD

➤ DID YOU KNOW...

➤ ...The Providence Steam Roller (1925) won New England's first NFL championship, but it is better known for three quirky league firsts. 1) It was the first NFL team to play its home games in a bicycle racing stadium; 2) it was the first NFL team to play a night game under the lights – they painted the ball white – and, 3) it was the first and only NFL team to play four regularly scheduled league games in six days (0-3-1).

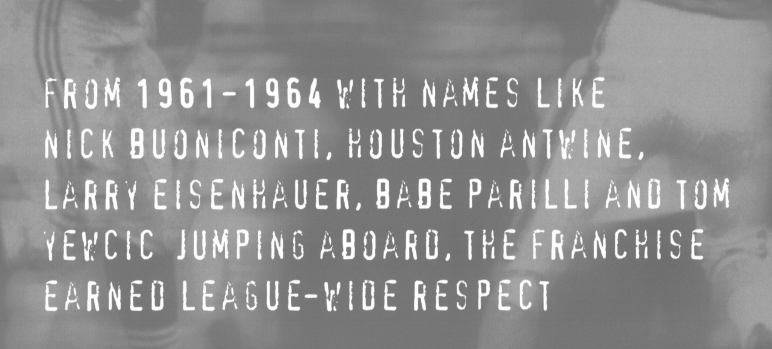

FROM 1961–1964 WITH NAMES LIKE NICK BUONICONTI, HOUSTON ANTWINE, LARRY EISENHAUER, BABE PARILLI AND TOM YEWCIC JUMPING ABOARD, THE FRANCHISE EARNED LEAGUE-WIDE RESPECT

WITH A 35-17-4 RECORD

ABOVE   Jim Lee Hunt   LEFT TO RIGHT   Nick Buoniconti, Houston Antwine, Larry Eisenhauer

KRAFT KEEPS PATRIOTS HOME

By Kevin Mannix, *Boston Herald*

After 40 years of begging for financial help from the public sector and searching for a home, the Patriots are New England's prodigal sons no longer. The opening of Gillette Stadium for the 2002 season was the final stage in the seemingly endless battle to build long-term stability. **1 0 > The off-season trade of Drew Bledsoe to the Bills** had people waxing poetic about how The Former Franchise saved the Patriots. Others felt that the arrival of Bill Parcells rescued the team from oblivion. In reality, the team was saved by its fourth owner, Robert Kraft. There were times when even he appeared to be overmatched by the political climate in Massachusetts. At one point, the ongoing battle to get financial support from the State House as well as a $1 billion offer from the state of Connecticut, led Kraft to sign a tentative agreement to move the team to Hartford. **2 0 > He bailed out of that commitment** when it became apparent that Connecticut would be unable to get the new facility built and ready for occupancy for the 2001 season, as was expected. **3 0 > Within months, Kraft's preference for building a new stadium in Foxborough** was assured by two developments: the NFL developed a new plan to lend money to teams building new stadiums, and the state voted more than $70 million for infrastructure around the site of the new (Gillette Stadium) facility. **4 0 > Until Kraft took over,** the team was owned by a dedicated Bostonian of limited means (Billy Sullivan), a business opportunist (Victor Kiam) and a caretaker carpetbagger (James Busch Orthwein) who got involved to protect earlier loans to Kiam that were in danger of being lost along with the rest of Kiam's investments. **5 0 > While Sullivan was adamant that the team had to remain in New England,** Kiam and Orthwein were actively trying to move. The NFL had to step in to keep Kiam from moving the team to Jacksonville before expansion. It took Kraft's intervention – as well as $171 million to buy the team – to keep Orthwein from moving the team to St. Louis, his hometown. The Gateway City, which had funded a new domed stadium at the time, had lost the Cardinals to Arizona and then lost a chance for an expansion team to Jacksonville and Baltimore. **6 0 > At the last minute,** as the specter of the team packing up for the trip west came closer, Kraft reached an agreement with Orthwein to buy the team. The stability is a welcome change from the early years. Franchise founder Billy Sullivan's team wound up playing home openers at every local venue except White Stadium as he inveigled and finagled his way through one financial plight after another. He borrowed money to buy the team. He borrowed money to make the payroll. He borrowed money to get his team a "permanent" home in Foxborough after striking out in attempts to find a home in Boston. **7 0 > It wasn't for lack of trying.** Sullivan's team played at Boston University, Boston College, Harvard Stadium and Fenway Park. In 1968, the team's "home" opener actually took place in Birmingham, Ala., because the Red Sox occupied Fenway that day. **8 0 > The construction of Schaefer Stadium,** the Cheapo Depot of NFL stadiums, in 1970 seemed to settle the uncertainty around the Pats future. By the end of the '80s, however, the creditors were at Sullivan's door again. Sullivan had spent millions in legal fees and payouts to minority stockholders to become the sole owner of the team in the 1970s. In the mid-'80s, his son Chuck lost more millions when he decided to promote a Michael Jackson tour, forcing the family to put the team up for sale. **9 0 > All that is in the past;** the Patriots

The Patriots family tree took root under its brash owner in 1960. The 35-man squad would labor under taskmaster Lou Saban, the franchise's first head coach, Mike Holovak as the first director of player personnel and Ed McKeever as the first general manager. Northwestern running back Ron Burton was the first-ever draft choice and Ed "Butch" Songin the first quarterback.

With no stadium to call its own, Boston's new football club reached a deal with Boston University to use the old Braves Field – its first of several foster homes and where it played for three seasons before renting from the Red Sox at Fenway Park.

The team's first training camp, held at the University of Massachusetts, saw players depart Amherst as quickly as they arrived. Some 350 men auditioned for that first 35-man roster. A 4-1 pre-season was highlighted by a dominating 43-6 win over the Denver Broncos in Providence, R.I.

As those same Broncos stampeded into Boston to kick off a new chapter in the city's heralded sports history for the 1960 season opener, excitement spread like an epidemic. But the euphoria was short-lived in the American Football League's first-ever game, as the Patriots stumbled, 13-10, just 35 days after walloping the same Denver club (news soon broke that Broncos coach Frank Filchock watched a Patriots practice and knew exactly what to expect). Their first win would come one week later against the New York Titans at the Polo Grounds.

The decade of the 1960s was not the ideal time to dent the Boston sports market. The beloved Red Sox owned the baseball town, the NBA's Celtics were draping the Boston Garden with championship banners, and the adored Bruins of Bobby Orr were just around the corner. Still, local fans grew devoted to an overachieving Patriots team lacking eye-popping athletes and star power, as the club began to experience rapid, but never ultimate, success. Players like Gino Cappelletti, Bob Dee, Tony Sardisco, Jim Lee Hunt, Jim Colclough, Larry Garron, George McGee and Ross O'Hanley were Patriot pioneers.

After a 5-9 inaugural season, the club entered its most prominent period of the '60s. From 1961-1964 with names like Nick Buoniconti, Houston Antwine, Larry Eisenhauer, Babe Parilli and Tom Yewcic jumping aboard, the franchise earned league-wide respect with a 35-17-4 record.

LEFT TO RIGHT DIRECTOR OF PLAYER PERSONNEL MIKE HOLOVAK, RON BURTON

> **DID YOU KNOW...**

> ...The nickname Patriots was chosen in a public contest in 1960 and artist Walter Pingree created the first logo, a tricorn hat. But soon after, the Patriots adopted Pat Patriot – a cartoon figure created by Phil Bissell.

> ...Lou Saban was the first head coach of the Patriots and his son, Nick Saban, worked under current head coach Bill Belichick when Belichick held that title with the Cleveland Browns.

DEAR MR. SULLIVAN: AS A RAPID (SIC
AND DELIGHTED WITH OUR NEV
I WOULD LIKE TO SUBMIT MY ORIGINAL

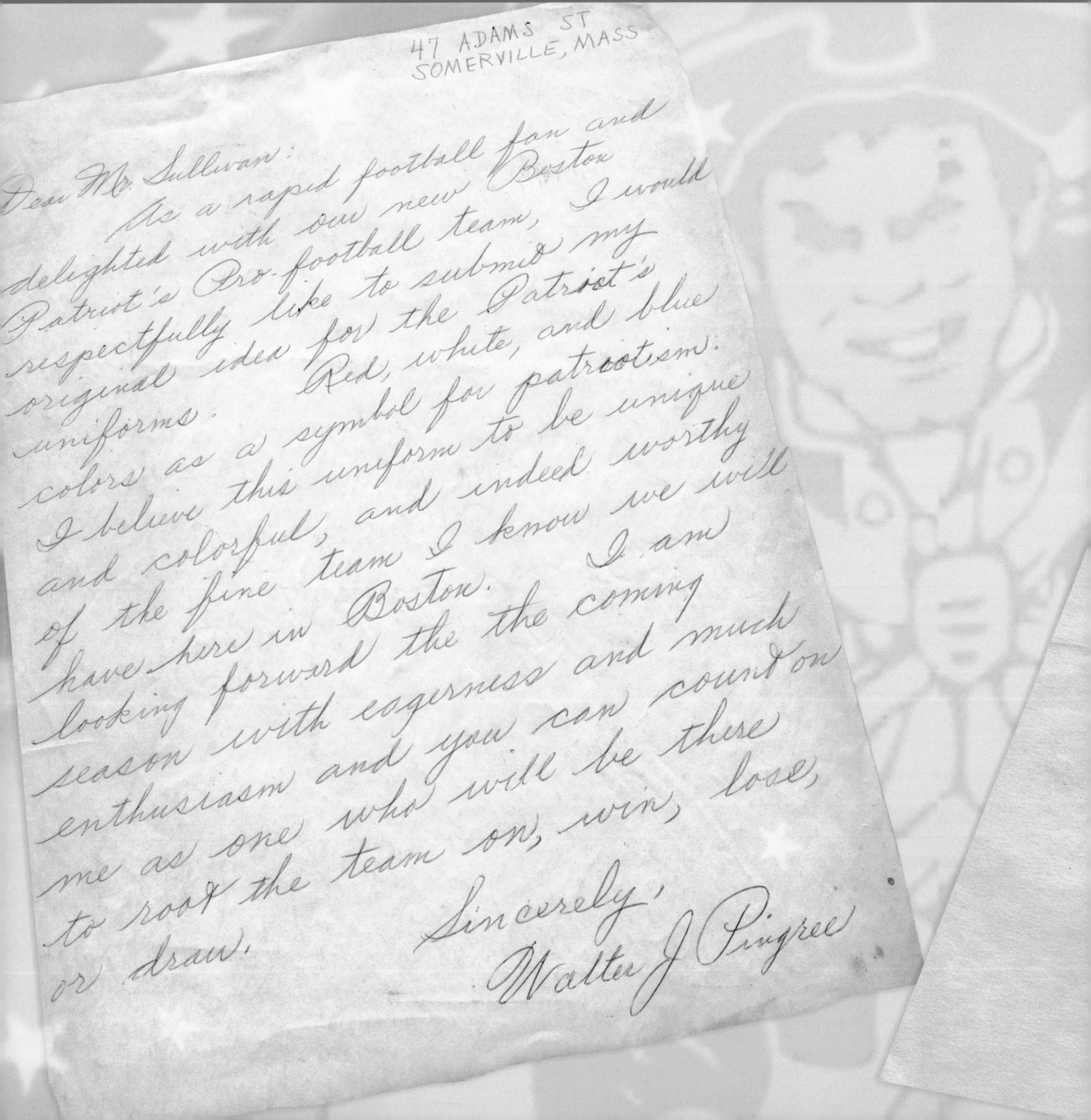

47 ADAMS ST
SOMERVILLE, MASS

Dear Mr. Sullivan:

As a rapid football fan and delighted with our new Boston Patriot's Pro-football team, I would respectfully like to submid my original idea for the Patriot's uniforms. Red, white, and blue colors as a symbol for patriotism. I believe this uniform to be unique and colorful, and indeed worthy of the fine team I know we will have here in Boston. I am looking forward the the coming season with eagerness and much enthusiasm and you can count on me as one who will be there to root the team on, win, lose, or draw.

Sincerely,
Walter J Pingree

METROPOLITAN COAL AND OIL COMPANY
EXECUTIVE OFFICES
53 STATE STREET
BOSTON 9, MASSACHUSETTS

WILLIAM H. SULLIVAN, JR.
PRESIDENT

Dear Mr. Pingree:

April 7, 1960

I can't begin to tell you how much we appreciate your thoughtfulness in reference to the uniform.

I am sure it will please you to learn that we are planning to adopt it, and, as the first step, we are having a uniform designed along the lines of that which you suggested.

A couple of changes have been made, but they are relatively slight. I think you will be happy to learn that the Boston Globe is taking a color picture of one of our players wearing the new uniform, and it will appear before long in that fine publication.

I will look forward to meeting you in the near future, but meanwhile, I do want you to know that we are very grateful for your thoughtfulness.

Sincerely,

Bill

WILLIAM H. SULLIVAN,

WHSjr/hj

Mr. Walter J. Pingree
Adams Street
Somerville, Massachusetts

Holovak, who took over for Saban in 1961, coached those teams. Saban's iron-fisted style had quickly worn thin, and Holovak's reputation as a player's coach breathed life into the Boston upstarts. They responded with the willingness to run through a wall for their new respected leader. The Houston Oilers proved to be a thorn in the Patriots side, capturing the first three AFL Eastern Division titles. Ironically, the Patriots broke through in 1963 – their first season playing at Fenway Park – with a 7-6-1 record that marked their worst in the four-year stretch from 1961-64, but offered their first taste of post-season football. The seven wins earned a tie with the Buffalo Bills atop the division, sending the teams to a playoff to determine which would represent the East for the AFL championship.

After soundly defeating the Bills, 26-8, at War Memorial Stadium in Buffalo, Boston made a transcontinental trip to San Diego, where it suffered the franchise's first major disappointment in a humiliating title game loss to the Chargers, 51-10.

The 1964 club was presumably the finest Patriots team of the decade and staked that claim with a 10-3-1 ledger, but a loss to the Bills in the final week cost them a chance to play host to San Diego for the championship.

Expectations predictably soared in 1965, but a 4-8-2 record upset Patriots fans who felt disappointed by their team and their own lofty expectations.

In 1966, Boston rebounded to make the decade's final playoff push with an 8-4-2 record and stood in first place after a hard-fought, 14-3, win over the Bills in Week 13. But a loss the following week to Joe Namath's Jets coupled with a Bills win gave the title to Buffalo in another bitterly disappointing finish. It was the end of the line for the '60s Patriots, who fell hard as the decade closed until bottoming out with a 2-12 record in 1970, the first season after the NFL-AFL merger. Holovak's devotion to his veteran players spelled the team's undoing as age and attrition caught up with Boston in the win column.

The dreadful 1970 season nearly burned to the ground before it started – literally. During a pre-season game versus Sonny Jurgensen's Washington Redskins at Boston College, the stands caught fire and the blaze sent fans pouring onto the field to safety in a true spectacle.

A year later, optimism was warranted for several reasons. First, Schaefer Stadium was constructed in Foxborough, Mass., for $6.7 million as the team's new "permanent" home, and played host to its first football game just 326 days after the September 23, 1970 groundbreaking. With the move south out of the city, Sullivan renamed his team the New England Patriots, turning it into a regional entity as it entered its new home with renewed hope.

> ## DID YOU KNOW...

> ...Gino Cappelletti became the first AFL player to score 1,000 points when he caught a 19-yard touchdown pass from Tom Sherman on November 10, 1968.

The first game in the new building was an August 15 pre-season affair with the New York Giants that is appropriately known more for the massive traffic jams in the stadium parking lots and along U.S. Route 1 than it is for the team's 20-14 win. In fact, many ticket-toting fans never saw the game because of the gridlock. Those who passed through the gates that memorable night saw the undisputed source for hope in 1971 in the arm of a hotshot, Heisman Trophy-winning rookie quarterback out of Stanford who was the first overall pick in the draft – Jim Plunkett.

Behind their new field general, the Patriots climbed out of the league's depths to a 6-8 record that, at the very least, showed improvement. Plunkett and the Patriots officially opened Schaefer nearly the same way Tom Brady and the 2001 Patriots closed Foxboro Stadium 31 years later – with a shocking win over the Oakland Raiders – the very team Plunkett would later lead to a pair of Super Bowl titles.

A championship in New England seemed inconceivable as Sullivan's Patriots flapped in the wind, devoid of football leadership from 1969 through the abysmal 3-11 season in 1972 until Chuck Fairbanks was hired to resurrect the franchise in 1973. Fairbanks was not Sullivan's first choice – Penn State's Joe Paterno and USC's John McKay were wooed – but the University of Oklahoma head coach was a splendid pick to head the Patriots as coach and *de facto* general manager.

ABOVE ORIGINAL OWNER WILLIAM "BILLY" SULLIVAN

LEFT TO RIGHT DARRYL STINGLEY, JIM PLUNKETT AND SAM CUNNINGHAM, STEVE GROGAN

SULLIVAN RENAMED HIS TEAM THE NEW
A REGIONAL ENTITY AS IT ENTERED

FOOTBALL'S VAGABONDS

By Richard Johnson, Curator, Sports Museum of New England

0 > *In their first dozen seasons* the Patriots took the field in their distinctive fire engine red home uniforms at seven stadiums in three states while playing in two leagues. Few teams in major professional sports have led a more nomadic existence. **10 >** *In 1960, Patriots founder Billy Sullivan* brought his fledgling team to the site of old Braves Field at Nickerson Field at Boston University. Not only had the BU/Braves Field site served for decades as home to countless college games such as many of the classic Boston College/Holy Cross contests in both football and baseball, but also as home to baseball's Braves it was headquarters to one of the two oldest continually operated pro sports franchises in North America. The site also had been home to three defunct pro football franchises, starting with the Boston Bulldogs of the first AFL in 1926, and their NFL namesakes in 1929; the NFL Braves, later known as the Boston Redskins following a move to Fenway Park, and the Washington Redskins after their relocation to the nation's capital in 1937. **20 >** *In 1963, 30 years after George Preston Marshall* moved his Redskins to Fenway Park, Sullivan moved his operation down Commonwealth Avenue. For most of the next six seasons the Patriots played at Fenway in the shadow of both the Green Monster and its baseball team. The 1967 "Impossible Dream" Red Sox forced the Pats to play the first of their two "home" road games as they faced the Chargers in San Diego twice within a month. The Red Sox also took precedence in 1968 when the Patriots adopted Legion Field in Birmingham, Alabama, in a 47-31 "home" loss to Joe Namath's Jets. **30 >** *In 1969 the Patriots moved* to Alumni Stadium at Boston College. Not only did the grandstand catch fire during a pre-season game at BC, but also the listless franchise was rumored to be moving anywhere from a proposed domed sports complex at Neponset Circle to Timbuktu. **40 >** *On April 4, 1970 the team announced* it had selected Foxborough, Mass., as the site of its new stadium. Harvard Stadium, site of previous exhibition and regular season games, would serve as interim home for their first season as members of the newly merged National Football League. **50 >** *Foxboro Stadium opened in August 1971,* less than a year after groundbreaking, with a memorable (and infamous) exhibition game against the New York Giants in which the stadium's toilets flooded concourses, and Route One traffic resembled Woodstock. In the 32 seasons that followed, the little stadium on Route One was known by three names – Schæfer Stadium, Sullivan Stadium and Foxboro Stadium. On January 19, 2002 the Patriots achieved their greatest home victory in the final game at Foxboro Stadium. **60 >** *In the shadow of the snowbound skeleton of Gillette Statium,* the team's newest home under construction next door, a frozen capacity crowd celebrated Adam Vinatieri's overtime kick that propelled his team to Pittsburgh, and finally glory at Super Bowl XXXVI in New Orleans. **70 >** *Forty-two seasons, seven homes,* and one Super Bowl championship later, it all seemed like a dream.

LEFT TO RIGHT

NICKERSON
FIELD
FENWAY PARK
HARVARD
STADIUM
FOXBORO
STADIUM

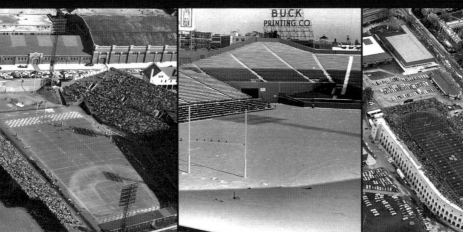

The decision paid immediate dividends with Fairbanks investing in a core of talent that included John Hannah, Sam Cunningham, Darryl Stingley, Ray Hamilton and Leon Gray. His first team struggled to stop opposing ground games and finished a paltry 5-9.

With a year of experience in his vault, Fairbanks banked on a three-linemen, four-linebacker defense – an alignment seldom used professionally in the early '70s, and he drafted linebacker Steve Nelson to facilitate the transition. The new Patriots exploded to a 5-0 start and sat at 6-1 after a comeback win over the Vikings – a game won when tight end Bob Windsor tore up his knee while twisting and pulling several defenders into the end zone on the final play.

Windsor's injury would be only one of the many that decimated the team in the weeks that followed, and the fast start was soon forgotten as New England lost six of its last seven for a demoralizing 7-7 final mark.

Several healthy bodies returned for 1975, but Plunkett suffered a shoulder injury during the pre-season and the Patriots never recovered, despite some impressive late season play from rookie quarterback Steve Grogan, out of Kansas State. At 15-27 after three years, Fairbanks' regime was being questioned.

He answered in 1976 – one of the Patriots all-time best seasons with one of its premier teams. Fairbanks traded Plunkett, inserted Grogan at quarterback and the inspiring Patriots dismantled some of the league's best teams in an 11-3 season that remains the franchise's best ever regular-season winning percentage. Along the way, New England overpowered the defending Super Bowl champion Steelers in Pittsburgh, handed a powerful Raiders squad its only defeat of the year and added wins over muscle-bound clubs in Baltimore and Miami.

ABOVE PUNTER AND QUARTERBACK TOM YEWCIC BREAKS AWAY FROM PURSUING JETS

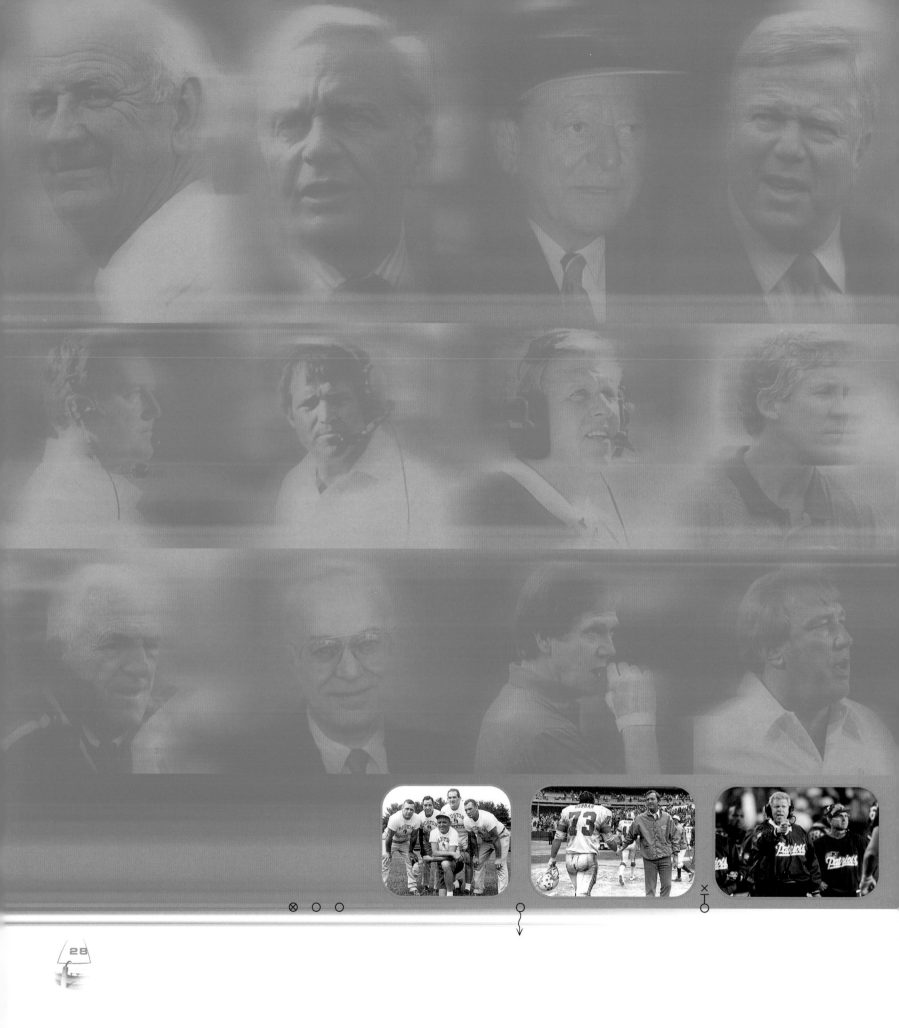

ABOVE. LEFT TO RIGHT BILLY SULLIVAN, VICTOR KIAM, JAMES ORTHWEIN, ROBERT KRAFT, CHUCK FAIRBANKS,
RON MEYER, BILL PARCELLS, PETE CARROLL, DICK MACPHERSON, ROD RUST, RAYMOND BERRY, RON ERHARDT
BELOW. LEFT TO RIGHT MIKE HOLOVAK AND STAFF, JOHN HANNAH AND CHUCK FAIRBANKS, BILL PARCELLS AND MIKE SWEATMAN

The season Patriots fans were waiting for finally arrived, and the team's second-ever playoff berth sent it to the West Coast to play the same Raider team it had dismantled 48-17 in Foxborough. The Patriots led 21-17 in Oakland when things went awry in a string of unfortunate and highly controversial penalties called against New England – the most infamous being the Phantom Roughing the Passer penalty called against Ray "Sugar Bear" Hamilton on a third-and-18 play inside the final two minutes. The Raiders took advantage of the early Christmas gifts and scored a touchdown with seconds remaining for a 24-21 Oakland win that would take 25 years to avenge.

With prosperity ahead for a young, talented team with greatness in sight, enthusiasm seated itself on the Patriots bandwagon only to be booted off by bitterness as the organization's second decade ended.

The period between 1976 and 1980 imprinted the also-ran image onto the psyches of Patriots fans as none of those capable units competed for a championship. Fast starts sputtered into late-season bewilderment and each campaign featured its own black mark. In 1977, star offensive linemen Hannah and Gray sat out the beginning of the season in a contract dispute.

In 1978, the 8-2 Patriots led the Oilers 23-0 in Week 11 only to lose 26-23 to start a 3-3 final six weeks that culminated in an AFC East title and the team's first-ever home playoff game – a 31-14 loss to that same Houston club. But the '78 season was noted for other reasons. Star wide receiver Darryl Stingley's career ended abruptly and tragically when a blow from Oakland's Jack Tatum left him paralyzed from the neck down.

It also was the last year of Fairbanks' reign, and his ousting is one of the franchise's innumerable bizarre moments. With the team in Miami preparing for the Monday night season finale, a story broke indicating his acceptance of a job with the University of Colorado – a story Fairbanks confirmed to Sullivan who suspended him on the spot, leaving his playoff-bound bunch without a leader. With offensive coordinator Ron Erhardt and his defensive counterpart Hank Bullough sharing head coaching duties, the Patriots were massacred 23-3. Fairbanks was reinstated for the playoff loss to Houston, his last game on New England's sideline.

In 1979, the cheers ended for the Patriots when they lost three of their final four games to finish 9-7 and miss the playoffs – a feat basically repeated in 1980 when a 6-1 start evaporated into a 10-6 finish and no post-season invitation. As the door to the 1980s creaked open, the Patriots reputation was firmly entrenched – they couldn't win, and they certainly didn't in 1981, turning in a feeble 2-14 performance.

➤ DID YOU KNOW...

➤ ...Schaefer Stadium was renamed Sullivan Stadium in 1983 and Foxboro Stadium in 1990 – the latter remaining until the stadium's demolition following the 2001 world championship season.

REPRESENTING THEM ALL

By Gino Cappelletti, Patriots alumnus and radio broadcaster

0> **The Super Bowl championship** was a wonderful culmination of 42 years of Patriots football, all of which I've been a part of in some way or another as a player, broadcaster and assistant coach. **10>** **Experience taught me through the years** that we were a franchise that always seemed to find a way to fall short. So many frustrating moments took place over those four decades that everyone wondered if a Patriots championship would ever happen. **20>** **This past season** was absolutely the most amazing year that we could ever experience, especially with the minimal expectations at the beginning of the year, and the team's stumble out of the gate, losing three of the first four. To have the Patriots come on as they did in such wonderful fashion with such a wonderful bunch of players was special. You had to like everything about this team – the personalities as well as the professionalism and the talent on the field. **30>** **The frustrations for this organization** started back in 1960, the very first year of the franchise. I attended the very first practice at the University of Massachusetts in Amherst and everything appeared to be negative back then. We had opportunities, but we couldn't get over the hump. That continued through the 1970s when I moved into the broadcast booth, culminating with the blown call against the Raiders in 1976 and Darryl Stingley's devastating injury two years later. **40>** **In the 1980s it was more of the same.** We rode a high into Super Bowl XX only to be pounded by the Bears, just as we had been by the Chargers in 1963 when we went to the AFL Championship game and lost 51-10. The Patriots always seemed to clear most of the hurdles, but not all. So many disappointing events prevented the team from doing what this year's was able to do. **50>** **That is why the 2001 team was so special.** All the bad luck or things that seemed to go wrong in four decades, all turned around in one season. Whatever the Patriots needed to happen, happened. They took full advantage of every opportunity.

60> **I can't say enough about this coaching staff.** I'm a player's player and I've always felt that the game belongs to the players, but the coaching staff was the difference in this team accomplishing what it did. The strategies they designed were brilliant and beautifully executed by the players. **70>** **The Super Bowl was an emotional experience.** When Adam Vinatieri ran out to kick the game-winning field goal, I totally expected him to make it. I anticipated the euphoria and I was ahead of myself. I started smiling and when he split the uprights, I just laughed like a big, happy kid. At that moment, I was thinking about all the players I had played with and know all over the country. **80>** **"How proud they must feel,"** was my first thought. That sense of pride in accomplishment is one of the greatest emotional sensations there is. **90>** **This cast of players** made it so easy to be proud. They did it.

LEFT TO RIGHT
STEVE NELSON
BABE PARILLI
JON MORRIS
TONY EASON

THE PATRIOTS OF THE MID-'80s WERE BUILT FOR SUCCESS

Mediocrity, characteristic near-misses and coaching changes ruled the day from 1982-1984. Erhardt, who replaced Fairbanks, was fired after the 1981 season and replaced by Ron Meyer from Southern Methodist University. Meyer eventually was caught up in a power struggle with the Sullivans and, in 1984, became the second Patriots coach along with Saban to be fired despite a winning record during the regular season. He was replaced by Hall-of-Fame wide receiver Raymond Berry, whose laid-back style hardly convinced the masses to store their pennies for Super Bowl tickets. Yet, with talent the likes of Stanley Morgan, Craig James, Tony Collins, Julius Adams, Andre Tippett, Don Blackmon, Raymond Clayborn, Irving Fryar, and Mosi Tatupu along with Hannah, Grogan, Nelson and Tony Eason, the Patriots of the mid-'80s were built for success.

Grateful Patriots fans finally had something to cheer about in 1985. New England "luck" continued to define itself that season when starting quarterback Tony Eason suffered an injury with his team already trying to dig out of a 2-3 hole. But with the venerable Grogan taking charge of the offense, the Patriots responded with six straight wins, only to see the veteran signal-caller himself lost for the regular season with a broken leg suffered in a Week 12 overtime loss to the Jets. With Eason back, New England won three of its last four, losing only a 3-point affair in Miami, before riding through the playoffs on a magic carpet. Improbable road wins over the Jets, Raiders and Dolphins earned the Patriots their first AFC Championship and a trip to New Orleans for Super Bowl XX.

Hope, of course, surrendered to frustration, and the Super Bowl elation ended when the Chicago Bears pummeled the Patriots into oblivion by a 46-10 count – the largest winning margin in the game's two-decade-old history. To worsen matters, a drug scandal involving several Patriots broke in the newspapers immediately after the game, effectively rubbing salt in the gaping wound left by the disheartening defeat. Even in Super Bowl consolation, the Patriots had found a way to tarnish their accomplishment.

31

As 1986 rolled around, the Super Bowl leftovers had enough left to contend, and New England finished atop the AFC East to make consecutive playoff appearances for the first time in the team's history. A post-season loss in Denver was the last playoff appearance for some time as front office mismanagement permeated the locker room and eroded the team's play.

Financial troubles stemming from an ill-advised investment in pop music star Michael Jackson's Victory Tour cost the Sullivan family stadium ownership and eventually contributed to the sale of the team itself. In 1988, Remington electric razor mogul Victor Kiam acquired the Patriots from Sullivan, thus commencing the worst era in franchise history. In what proved a major coup, Robert Kraft thankfully outbid Kiam for Sullivan Stadium ownership – a power play that would eventually aid his purchase of the Patriots.

But Kiam's tenure as owner was abysmal. With poor drafting contributing to an overall ineptitude in the organization, the Patriots floundered into obscurity, hitting an all-time performance low in 1990 when Rod Rust – in his only season as head coach – captained a 1-15 sinking ship. The darkest moment during that 1990 season, believe it or not, came off the field when a few players were charged with sexually harassing a *Boston Herald* reporter during an interview in the Patriots locker room.

Syracuse Head Coach Dick MacPherson replaced Rust, but won only eight games in two seasons, including a 2-14 season in 1992 that cost him his job. Earlier in 1992, controlling interest of the team changed hands again with James Busch Orthwein buying out Kiam. Rumors had Orthwein set to move the team to his native St. Louis, but the Patriots had a lease with Kraft to play in Foxboro Stadium – an arrangement that kept the team home and allowed Kraft to move in and acquire the club in 1994.

The direction of the franchise was changing and Kraft would eventually oversee the finishing touches. But it was Orthwein who hired the popular Bill Parcells as his head coach and it was Parcells who drafted Washington State quarterback Drew Bledsoe with the first pick in the 1993 draft. Those two moves were as significant as any in team history, as both helped save the franchise from its darkest hour.

The team showed mild improvement in 1993 and was 3-6 in 1994 when the franchise's fortunes began changing. Riding Bledsoe's cannon right arm, New England won seven straight games to end the 1994 season and qualify for the playoffs for the first time since 1986. Amazingly, the streak commenced with Bledsoe completing 45-of-70 passes – both NFL records – for 426 yards in a come-from-behind overtime win over the Vikings. With Parcells and Bledsoe in place along with players like Ben Coates, Willie McGinest and Bruce Armstrong, the reconstruction was well under way.

The club's second AFC Championship arrived in 1996. With offensive weapons Curtis Martin and Terry Glenn and defensive stalwarts Ty Law, Ted Johnson and Lawyer Milloy in the mix, the Patriots had the proper ingredients to land them back in New Orleans for a second shot at Super Bowl glory. Home playoff wins over Pittsburgh and Jacksonville pitted New England in Super Bowl XXXI against the league's best team and the heavy favorite Green Bay Packers, who waltzed past the upset-minded Patriots, 35-21, leaving New England 0-for-2 in the big game.

On-field success did little to mask some off-field duress, and a feud between Kraft and Parcells led to a bitter break-up. The Patriots turned to former San Francisco 49ers defensive coordinator Pete Carroll to replace Parcells and while he guided the talented Patriots back to the playoffs in 1997 and 1998, decline was obvious as 11-5 fell off to 10-6, 9-7 and worse. When Carroll's club faded to 8-8 and out of the playoffs in 1999, his run was over.

When Bill Belichick was hired as the team's 14th head coach in 2000, the New England faithful hardly greeted him with open arms. Belichick, who was on the Patriots 1996 AFC Champion coaching staff as an assistant, set about redesigning the roster over his first two seasons, and a 5-11 record in his first year only created more doubters.

Would that slow start doom the dour Belichick, and his team, to more upheaval and unrest? The 2001 season would answer that question, in a way no one could have foreseen.

PATRIOTS HALL OF FAME

THEY ARE BRUCE ARMSTRONG (78), ANDRE TIPPETT (56), GINO CAPPELLETTI (20), MIKE HAYNES (40)

AVE BEEN INDUCTED INTO THE PATRIOTS HALL OF FAME; EIGHT OF THEM HAVE THEIR NUMBERS RETIRED.
TEVE NELSON (57), JOHN HANNAH (73), JIM LEE HUNT (79) AND BOB DEE (89)

FROM LEFT TO RIGHT
* INDICATES A PRO FOOTBALL HALL OF FAMER

GINO CAPPELLETTI

JOHN HANNAH *

MIKE HAYNES *

NICK BUONICONTI *

BOB DEE

STEVE GROGAN

JIM LEE HUNT

STEVE NELSON

BABE PARILLI

ANDRE TIPPETT

BRUCE ARMSTRONG

CHAPTER 2

A LINE IS DRAWN

IT WAS A TYPICAL, FRIGID NEW ENGLAND

WINTER THURSDAY. AT 4:01 P.M. ON

JANUARY 27, 2000, PATRIOTS OWNER

ROBERT KRAFT MANEUVERED HIS DEEP

BLUE LEXUS INTO A CRAMPED FOXBORO

STADIUM PARKING LOT AND EMERGED

BESIDE THE MAN HE WAS TO NAME

AS THE 14TH HEAD COACH OF THE

NEW ENGLAND PATRIOTS.

THE PRO BOWL CONNECTION

0> **Bill Belichick loves to use visuals** or cite examples to deliver a message and during the June 2001 mini-camp, the Patriots head coach addressed his players' desire for glory and stardom and in the process offered another steadfast reason to focus on team football – its results are crucial for individual recognition. Belichick read off this list of names:

Donnie Abraham > Sam Adams > Trace Armstrong > Matt Birk > Daunte Culpepper > Hugh Douglas > Mark Fields > La'Roi Glover > Martin Gramatica > Brian Griese > Robert Griffith > Torry Holt > Brad Hopkins > Joe Horn > Tim Ruddy > Larry Izzo > Lincoln Kennedy > Chad Lewis > Brock Marion > Derrick Mason > Donovan McNabb > Steve McNair > Keith Mitchell > Samari Rolle > Rod Smith > Ron Stone > Matt Stover > Korey Stringer > Jason Taylor > Jeremiah Trotter

1|0> **"What do these 30 players have in common?"** he asked his team, with no response forthcoming. "All 30 made their first trip to the Pro Bowl in 2000 and all were on playoff teams in 2000. They didn't make it because every single scheme and game plan revolved around these individuals, but because their teams embraced a program, chemistry gained momentum and they won. Almost seven of every 10 Pro Bowlers came off playoff rosters." **2|0>** **The message sank in.** The Patriots sent no one to the Pro Bowl during their 5-11 season in 2000, but last year Ty Law, Lawyer Milloy, Tom Brady and Troy Brown all earned trips to Hawaii – Brady and Brown for the first time.

> THE CLASS OF 2001

Player	Position	College	Round	Overall
Richard SEYMOUR	DL	Georgia	1	6
Matt LIGHT	OL	Purdue	2	48
Brock WILLIAMS	CB	Notre Dame	3	86
Kenyatta JONES	OL	South Florida	4	96
Jabari HOLLOWAY	TE	Notre Dame	4	119
Hakim AKBAR	S	Washington	5	163
Arther LOVE	TE	South Carolina State	6	180
Leonard MYERS	CB	Miami	6	200
Owen POCHMAN	P	BYU	7	216
T.J. TURNER	LB	Michigan State	7	239

"YOU WIN AS A TEAM, YOU LOSE AS A TEAM;
YOU MAKE PICKS AS A TEAM"

— ROBERT KRAFT

Twenty-four days earlier, the 1999 season had concluded with the team excluded from the playoffs for the first time in four years, and Kraft exited the same lot having just fired Pete Carroll.

With little more than a firm handshake consummating the deal, Bill Belichick was introduced to the media as the man to guide the Patriots back to prominence, to break them out of the miniature Ice Age that periodically blankets Patriots Nation.

The announcement was hardly met with jubilation. There were no ovations, no pep rallies, no motivational speeches and most of all, no guarantees – just a renewed hope based on core football principles – discipline, hard work, toughness and

teamwork. As Kraft and Belichick sat side-by-side at a long table draped in a milk-white tablecloth and littered with microphones and tape recorders, the two spoke of a common goal for a franchise in search of football direction.

"Bill doesn't have a big ego. You win as a team, you lose as a team; you make picks as a team. That's the culture we want around here," Kraft said.

The post-Super Bowl XXXI Patriots were in steady decline, and Kraft hand-picked the man to rebuild his franchise, hoping to match the torrid pace with which his new $325 million stadium, Gillette Stadium, was rising just a kickoff away from where the two men sat.

39

ABOVE ROBERT KRAFT ANNOUNCES THE HIRING OF HEAD COACH BILL BELICHICK

THEY SOUGHT PLAYERS WHO WERE WILLING
SPECIAL TEAMS PERFORMERS.

Kraft faced a difficult decision to surrender a compensatory first-round draft choice to the rival New York Jets – to whom Belichick was contractually obligated – for his new coach's services, but the owner rested on experience when endorsing the exchange.

"I thought about the Robert Edwards situation," the owner explained, "and about the uncertainty that we all have with draft picks." Edwards was a former first-round selection and potential star who injured his knee after one season and never played again for New England. With Belichick, Kraft felt secure despite having to finalize the deal with his former employee and new rival, Bill Parcells, now the Jets general manager.

The owner never blinked. Bill Belichick was his man. Hiring the former Browns head coach came off a blueprint not unlike those he pored over every day as the plans for the team's new stadium took shape. Belichick had New England and football coursing through his veins; he had attended high school at Phillips Academy in Andover, Mass., and lettered in lacrosse and football at Wesleyan University in Middletown, Conn. He had turned in a quarter century on the NFL sidelines, as a defensive guru for almost 20 years and as head coach for five, and had served as assistant head coach in New England under Bill Parcells in 1996.

The supreme compliment was on permanent display at the Pro Football Hall of Fame in Canton – the defensive game plan he put together for the New York Giants victory over Buffalo in Super Bowl XXV. Still, with this pedigree, some wagging tongues claimed he was Xs and Os crazy, a coaching robot.

Not included in the mob of naysayers was a legion of All-Star NFL signal-callers who had to deal with Belichick on Sunday afternoons. They recognized quality: "I gave up a long time ago trying to figure out whether I'm going to get zoned or manned or blitzed. Bill Belichick changes it every single week." – Dan Marino. "I thought he was a very good coach when I was at Cleveland. All the experience he absorbed in his last few years there is going to make him a better coach." – Vinny Testaverde. "You don't know how they're going to line up. Are they going to be in a five-linebacker set with 20 DBs? What are they going to do? They make you do your homework." – Doug Flutie.

Defenders echoed those sentiments.

Kraft knew he was on solid ground when he negotiated for Belichick. "For a number one draft choice, we can bring in a man who I feel certain will do something rather than with the uncertainty of the draft pick," he explained. Thus began the championship movement that culminated in a Super Bowl XXXVI victory and continues into the foreseeable future.

Few beyond Kraft believed an instant about-face would happen in January 2000, especially with the financial hardship staring down Belichick as he sought to reshape his new squad while fitting what he already had under the salary cap. With his hands tied and no first-round draft choice to infuse life into a dormant locker room, Belichick set about signing free agents like Aaron Bailey, Raymont Harris, Eric Bjornson, Antonio Langham, Sale Isaia, Joe Andruzzi, Bobby Hamilton and Grant Williams, many of whom never made it to the 2001 season.

His first draft, which would show quality a year or so down the road, landed future contributors Greg Robinson-Randall, J.R. Redmond, Antwan Harris, Tom Brady and Patrick Pass.

HAD EXPERIENCE AND CHARACTER, AND MOST IMPORTANTLY, LOVED FOOTBALL

"Bill (Belichick) is the best game day coach I've ever been around. His staff also deserves credit. They do a great job of keeping things calm and telling you what's going to happen." – then-Jets linebacker Bryan Cox. "I can't say enough about him. He's by far the best coach I've ever had in my career. I don't think I'll ever get another coach that can call plays and defenses like that." – cornerback Aaron Glenn.

It became glaringly obvious that an immediate turnaround was implausible as Belichick patiently and methodically began molding the team in his own image. The draft had his thumbprint on it, but when his first pick, tackle Adrian Klemm, suffered an injury in a spring mini-camp, a "here-we-go-again" mentality crept back into the populace.

41

"I CAN'T SAY ENOUGH ABOUT HIM
HE'S BY FAR THE BEST COAC

'VE EVER HAD IN MY CAREER"

— AARON GLENN

|0> **Bill Belichick's month-old off-season** focused on improving a football team in desperate need of upgrading. Who would the Patriots draft with the sixth pick? What free agents would they target? How would they fill all the holes? How would they better 5-11? |0> **Belichick huddled in his Foxboro Stadium corner office** for countless hours, dissecting film of prospective Patriots, seeking answers. One solution fell into his arms on February 1, 2001 with the arrival of colleague and confidant Romeo Crennel. 2|0> **In his first season as the Patriots mentor,** Belichick had doubled as defensive coordinator, entrusting no one with the installation of his system. Crennel, meanwhile, was dutifully occupied as a first-year coordinator for the Cleveland Browns. A Browns coaching change afforded Belichick an otherwise unavailable opportunity to obtain a valuable assistant, and he needed neither film nor interview to enlist Crennel as his new defensive leader. 3|0> **"There isn't a coach I respect and trust more** than Romeo," Belichick said upon the hiring. "Our relationship goes back 20 years. Nobody knows my defensive system better than Romeo. We've coached together a long time, and the system is derived from the people we've been around for so many years. 4|0> **"I'm really excited.** You come to work each day, especially at this time of year, and every day you hope you can make the team better than it was. Today is a very easy day for me because I know we're a better football team than we were yesterday." 5|0> **Belichick and Crennel shared 10 years** on the New York Giants staff (1981-1990), winning two Super Bowls while compiling a 90-61 record. They came together again in 1996, helping the Patriots to Super Bowl XXXI and, after leaving New England, both worked for the New York Jets for three seasons, advancing as far as the AFC Championship game in 1998's 12-4 season. 6|0> **Crennel was asked** why he and Belichick could lead the Patriots back to the Super Bowl. "Because we've won everywhere we've been together," was the simple explanation. "We've been able to work a system and get the players that work well within it – team guys who work hard and play hard," Crennel explained. 7|0> **"Bill, Charlie Weis and I know each other.** We're on the same page and we know what it takes and how to go about putting guys in position to make plays and have a chance to win."

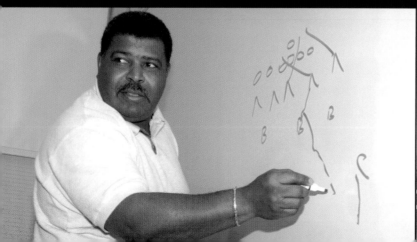

During the pre-season, a scrawny Brady played sparingly and gave no indication of becoming the clutch, mistake-free quarterback who would lead the franchise to its first world title. In 2000, expressing such thoughts was enough to warrant a straitjacket.

Thus with a barebones talent pool, exacerbated by inexperience and a dearth of leadership, Belichick's first Patriots team performed inconsistently and finished a miserable and predictable 5-11. The season served more to arrest decay than it did to rebuild, but total reconstruction began the moment reserve quarterback Michael Bishop's Hail Mary pass fluttered harmlessly to the earth on the last play of a 2000 season-ending loss to Miami.

With salary cap constraints still hampering Belichick's shopping freedom in 2001, he and personnel director Scott Pioli instituted an "intelligent shoppers" policy. They identified and targeted their type of players – those willing to work hard, sacrifice themselves and prepare to win. The 2001 team was going to be improved in areas of skill, leadership, experience and effort, even if it wasn't laden with high-priced superstars.

ABOVE Matt Light contributed as a starter in his rookie season LEFT TO RIGHT Director of Player Personnel Scott Pioli and COO Andy Wasynczuk, Mike Compton, Terrell Buckley

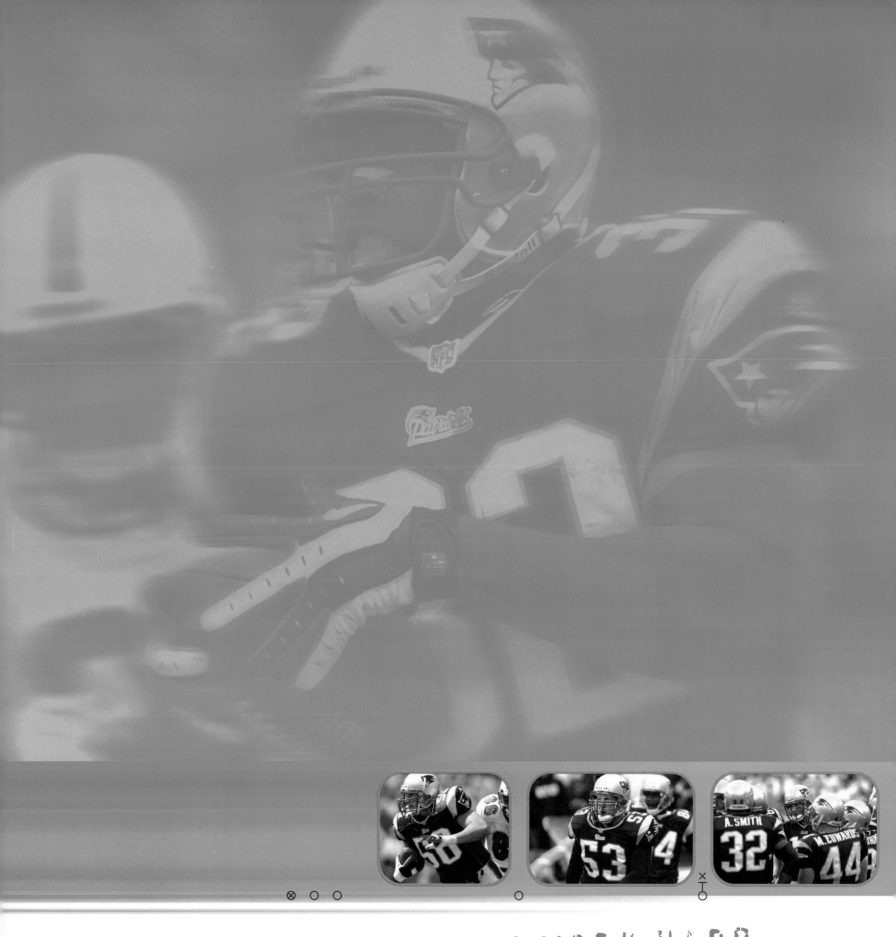

— THOSE WILLING TO WORK HARD,
SACRIFICE THEMSELVES

ABOVE ANTOWAIN SMITH CARRIES **LEFT TO RIGHT** MIKE VRABEL, LARRY IZZO, SMITH
WITH TOM BRADY AND MARC EDWARDS, TROY BROWN, ANTHONY PLEASANT

The spring's free agent transactions were met with the same disinterest as those of the prior off-season as critics and fans alike remained unimpressed. Few expected significant contributions from Larry Izzo, Mike Vrabel, Matt Stevens, Marc Edwards, Anthony Pleasant, Terrance Shaw, Bert Emanuel, Mike Compton, Damon Huard or David Patten – all of whom came aboard during the NFL Doldrums, that period between the March onset of free agency and the April draft.

Post-draft, pre-training camp acquisitions included more of the same: Charles Johnson, Torrance Small, Johnny McWilliams, Riddick Parker, Antowain Smith and Terrell Buckley. This lackluster list may have failed to encourage enthusiasm and championship aspirations, but no reporter, coach, owner or scout could accurately predict how the players would bond and unite into the purest form of team.

One local newspaper wondered, derisively, "Where's the beef?" when Compton and Patten – two prominent contributors in 2001 – came aboard. That same publication called the Patriots shopping spree "Wal-Martesque" adding, "Value shopping, they call it. Quantity, for sure, but the quality is yet to be seen."

Another outlet offered this critique of the Patriots off-season progress: "The Patriots apparently feel that going for a bunch of inexpensive players rather than one or two big-ticket items is the best approach to building a championship team. For downtrodden and downhearted Patriots fans, however, there is a distinct 'Is that all there is?' feel to the recent maneuvers. Quantity is there, but there appears to be a lack of quality."

That insidious skepticism, which lingered all season despite the team's eventual success, only served to motivate a Patriots club that leaned on the "lack of respect" theme for inspiration. Such disrespect even rained down from the league schedule-makers who gave the Patriots the Week 17 bye usually reserved for teams with poor prospects.

The Patriots maintained short-term focus and moved onward. While pre-Belichick holdovers were either allowed to leave or were nudged out the revolving door, Belichick and Pioli adhered to their blueprint. With goals of creating a financial middle class on the roster as well as improving it from the bottom up, they sought players who were willing special teams performers, had experience and character, and most importantly, loved football.

Their model emphasized special teams play, and Belichick used starters and reserves alike to make sure his squad excelled in the kicking game – a phase that contributed greatly to a Super Bowl title. Additionally, without sending blank checks to overrated free agents, the Patriots targeted four- and five-year veterans who were still on the upside of their careers and had starting-caliber ability.

The ongoing improvement process continued into training camp when linebackers Bryan Cox and Roman Phifer, two valuable veterans who had played for Belichick with the Jets, boarded the ship willing to assert themselves.

AND PREPARE TO WIN

0> *Still on the street* when 2001 NFL training camps kicked off in sweltering summer heat, Bryan Cox and Roman Phifer waited patiently for the phone to ring. Two dependable veteran linebackers with 22 years experience and 1,942 tackles between them waited for someone, anyone, with NFL acumen, to summon them to detestable two-a-days and dorm rooms. **10>** With salary cap constraints jettisoning aging players league-wide, the two bided their time. Bill Belichick knew both players well from his days with the New York Jets and was not about to field his team for the 2001 season opener while the two capable, diligent, experienced graybeards remained unemployed. **20>** *As July gave way to August,* both joined the Patriots already-in-progress training camp at Bryant College over a four-day span – Cox on July 31 and Phifer on August 3. Both hustled back to work to prepare for an 11th season, both still in search of a first championship. **30>** *Cox hauled his reputation like his luggage.* He was vocal. He was candid. His emotions were readily accessible to his teammates, with whom he was more than willing to share. The Patriots needed his authoritative guidance. **40>** *"My experience with Bryan has been very positive,"* Belichick said. "When I was with the Jets he was a strong leader on that team. Bryan is a smart guy. He's well-respected for the way he plays the game and I have a lot of respect for him for the way he approaches the game and his commitment to team football." **50>** *Phifer, conversely, was quiet and unassuming,* but business-like to say the least. His signing was practically invisible, but his play was eye-catching. The 92 tackles, two sacks, two fumble recoveries, and another pair of forced fumbles and an interception he would deliver during the season were immense for a team in need of such contribution. **60>** *"I think he exceeded expectations,"* defensive coordinator Romeo Crennel said in reference to Phifer. "I don't think we anticipated he'd play as much as he did. He played most of the defensive plays, he played special teams and he played several positions. He was a playmaker, he was consistent and was a versatile, valuable member of our team." **70>** *But his experience,* field presence and approach to the game were as vital as any statistic, simply not measurable on paper – just like Cox and the 2001 Patriots themselves. "They're both professionals," Crennel added. "Bryan is a more fiery leader and has been one everywhere he's been. Phifer is good in the locker room, but he's a quiet leader." **80>** *When the last gun sounded on a super season,* and the team waded off the Superdome field through an avalanche of confetti and congratulations, Phifer and Cox were among numerous MVPs – Most Valuable Patriots.

TRAINING CAMP
ADDITIONS
ROMAN PHIFER
AND BRYAN COX
CONTRIBUTED
MIGHTILY TO
THE DEFENSE

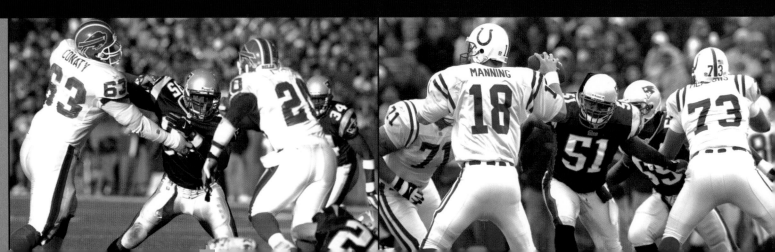

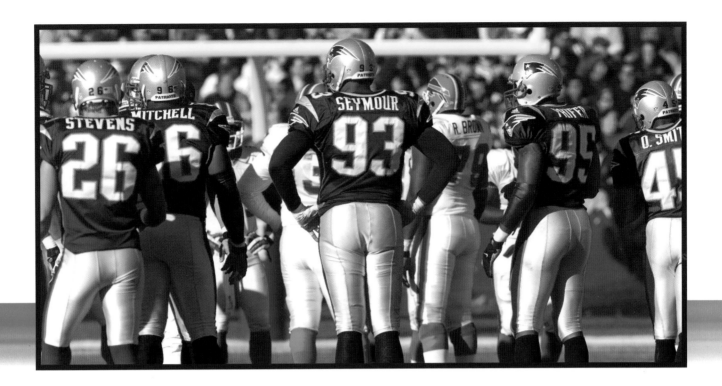

Few prognosticators bought into the team-building strategy. The media also condemned the Patriots April selections of defensive lineman Richard Seymour and other draft picks as it piled on Belichick, who was perceived to be treading water following a wretched first year. The experts insisted that a wide receiver was the team's foremost draft priority after a 2000 season in which the offense struggled and quarterback Drew Bledsoe seemed weaponless in his effort to alleviate the problem. When the Patriots bypassed Michigan wideout David Terrell in favor of Seymour, the media hatchets started swinging.

"Not getting a wide receiver in the first round was bad enough. Belichick then compounded the mistake by sitting back and letting all the second-level wide receivers get scooped up before he had a chance to present one to Bledsoe in the second round," one publication trumpeted. "Rather than making a trade to get one of the secondary receivers, members of what was considered to be one of the deepest drafts for the position in memory, Belichick moved down to get more picks – and then took a slow offensive lineman (Matt Light).

"His goal throughout this particular marathon appeared to be the addition of depth. Championship teams do that. Winning teams do that. Teams that are 5-11 and have missed the playoffs the last two seasons should look for talent that will make them more productive, not deeper."

The astute tandem of Belichick and Pioli understood the value of depth in an injury-riddled league and knew team toughness started nearest the football, which is why they emphasized the rebuilding of the offensive and defensive lines upon their arrival, hence the Seymour and Light selections in the first two rounds of the 2001 draft. Both players started almost the entire season.

"We're not going to stop improving our team," is all Belichick would say in response to questions on his decision-making.

The Patriots front office, its convictions secure, politely ignored the cynics while maintaining a consistent approach predicated on preparation.

Next stop, Smithfield, Rhode Island and Bryant College, to prepare for a new season.

49

CHAPTER 3

WANTED: WINNERS

THERE IS SOMETHING SPECIAL ABOUT

THE FIRST DAY OF TRAINING CAMP.

AS THE MORNING SUN RISES OVER

THE SPARKLING, DEW-SOAKED GREEN

PRACTICE FIELDS AT BRYANT COLLEGE

IN SMITHFIELD, R.I., THE DAWN OF

A NEW SEASON CLUTCHES THE HOPES

AND DREAMS OF SUPER BOWL GLORY

RESERVED FOR ONLY ONE TEAM.

The joy of it all is that every team, at 0-0, wonders, "Why not us?"

One hour later, that scene is shattered. As it rises, the sun becomes an unrelenting presence in the sky; the diamond-like dew evaporates, contributing to life-sucking humidity that leaves all participants desiccated and exhausted. "Why not us?" may still be in the air, but these athletes will have to grind it out and go beyond what they previously thought were their physical limits.

It is why the tenth sprint is run as hard as the first, why a Pro Bowl performer like Lawyer Milloy races downfield in punt coverage as relentlessly and recklessly as the rookie long-shot from No Chance University and why the sweat, soreness and suffering are worthwhile and some days, even rewarding.

Painted white lines, tackling dummies, blocking sleds, camera towers, moving trucks, metal bleachers, sponsorship signage, water coolers, food vendors and spectator tents stand at attention, ready for inspection, waiting for the barking of NFL drill sergeants to commence, for 89 pro football hopefuls striving to be the best to trample the manicured grass in boot camp drills.

PLAYTIME IS OVER. FOOTBALL SEASON IS HERE

ABOVE LEFT LAWYER MILLOY UNDER THE WATCHFUL EYE OF STRENGTH AND CONDITIONING COACH MIKE WOICIK

Playtime is over. Training camp means double sessions in stifling heat and protracted nighttime meetings and film sessions. It means studying a four-inch-thick playbook in a cramped, airless dorm room on a cot ill-designed for six-feet, four-inch 300-pound behemoths, and it means bonding with teammates.

Football season is here.

For the New England Patriots there are other symbols of camp life. The sigh that responds to the picturesque drive up the hill from Route 7 past the college security booth. The spray of the geyser-like fountain greets campus visitors, and refreshes those lucky enough to drive with the top down.

Everywhere there are familiar, eye-catching sights: the rotunda building, the pleasant blonde woman supervising the cafeteria with a smile, the fish swimming beside the campus bridge awaiting morsels of food, and the legendary archway that is allegedly haunted.

Oh, and the walking, lots of walking. The dormitories sit on one side of campus and the practice fields on the other, with the temporary locker room serving as a halfway house. Before and after practice, players march to and fro about the length of five football fields. Some veterans tool around on motorized scooters to save their legs, but the rookies all walk.

O CAMP AS A "NECESSARY EVIL"

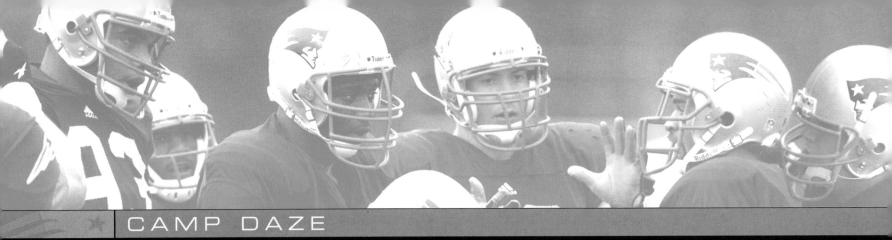

CAMP DAZE

By Richard Seymour, Patriots defensive lineman

Training camp was a time for me to really understand the concept of the defense because in college you can play on raw talent, but not in the pros. I came in a couple of days late because my contract wasn't signed and when I didn't know my plays, I would hear, "Maybe if you were here on time, you'd know that." **I remember being tired** and Bryan Cox saying, "C'mon big fella, we need to step it up another notch today." He would tell me that the days you don't want to be out there – which is a lot – are the times when you get better, and they are the times you'll look back to and appreciate when you're winning. **I didn't know camp would be as long** and as monotonous as it was. It was more than a month of going out twice a day in the heat. I wasn't as prepared mentally as I needed to be. I thought it would be cooler in New England, but it was hotter up here at that time than it was back home in South Carolina. **When the Giants** came for inter-squad practices, it really helped us. The first practice they really got the best of us, and it forced us step it up and become stronger and closer because we didn't appreciate them coming in and pushing us around. With another team in your face, you'll turn it up a notch. You get tired of hitting your own guys, which I also did plenty of. I didn't know what to expect when I first went out there, but I realized quickly I could play at this level and I probably got in more fights during camp than anybody else. I think I fought all the offensive linemen. **Camp also featured** some of the normal rookie harassment. Every other day, the rookies had to get up during meetings and entertain the veterans with songs or skits. Leonard Myers was the best because he can dance. We rookies got our own back, too. We would always make fun of Ty Law and Lawyer Milloy – how they talked in practice or in the meeting rooms. They were so confident that they'd be telling the coach, "Nah, that's not the way it's supposed to go." They knew it all and they would get into it with each other arguing how a play should be executed. So we made jokes about that. One rookie would be the coach and then two guys would sit in the classroom imitating Ty and Lawyer arguing about how things were supposed to be. It was funny stuff. They also shaved our heads and they let it go until the last day so we would have shiny domes for the first part of the regular season. When you finish camp, you want to get out and relax a little bit, but we had to go out bald. **Overall, it was a necessary experience** and a good environment to build a team, especially if the work was put in. The guys on this team made me feel at home by asking about my family, my home and my upbringing. They wanted to know more about me and it showed they were human beings rather than just sports machines that play football. They were caring people who wanted to know about me. That's one of the reasons our team has such terrific chemistry.

TYPICAL SEYMOUR DAY   **0700** Wake up, clean up and go to breakfast   **0800** Walk to training room to get taped up   **0820** Dress for practice   **0840** Walk out to field to stretch and prepare   **0850** Practice begins   **1100** Practice ends; carry veterans' pads back to locker room   **1130** Eat lunch; drink lots of water to stay hydrated   **1145** Get back to dorm room, get off my feet and rest or sleep; drink water   **1400** Walk back to training room for taping   **1420** Dress for practice; usually shorts in the afternoon without full pads   **1440** Walk out to practice to stretch and prepare   **1450** Second practice session begins   **1700** Practice ends; run sprints   **1730** Supper   **1800** Meetings   **2030** Snack and go back to dorm to relax, shoot pool or watch TV   **2200** Go to bed and get ready to do it all over again

Patriots great Bruce Armstrong often referred to camp as a "necessary evil" adding, "you can't get from A to C without going through B."

The Patriots 2001 training camp, however, found itself stuck on A – for Adversity. It is how the players and coaches tackled that adversity that earned them an A on their training camp report card. Some incidents were mere blips on the season's radar screen while others were sinkholes waiting to swallow vulnerable souls, of which there were relatively few. Bryant College proved to be its own kind of obstacle course.

If hope seems eternal for NFL clubs in July, that of running back Robert Edwards was undoubtedly infinite. Two years rehabilitating a reconstructed left knee were put to an immediate test – as in the grueling pre-training camp conditioning test, which Edwards failed once before passing. But not even Edwards' unwavering will could thrust him into intense camp competition at running back. A strained groin muscle suffered the first full-squad workday left him outside the fray. He was eventually released.

A TRUE VOYAGE

0> **The 1914-16 Antarctic Voyage of Sir Ernest Shackleton** – its horrors and ultimate triumphs – delivers a powerful message of survival, endurance, teamwork and human spirit. Shackleton's story, to a relative degree, mirrors that of the 2001 Patriots in that no respectable scriptwriter could possibly embellish the amazing tale of hardships overcome en route to ultimate success. **10>** **Understanding his club's low expectations and his obligation** to prevent negativity from infiltrating his locker room, Patriots Head Coach Bill Belichick organized a training camp field trip to Providence, Rhode Island's Feinstein IMAX Theatre for a viewing of Shackleton's Antarctic Adventure. **20>** **The epic story details** Shackleton's failed bid to cross Antarctica. Out of bitter defeat emerged a heroic saga of the amazing survival of 28 courageous men. Rather than just another training camp, team-building trip, Patriots players were treated to a wonderful parable on overcoming adversity through determination. **30>** **Shackleton's voyage diverted** toward disaster when the frozen sea imprisoned his ship, The Endurance, thousands of miles from civilization without radio contact. The force of the glacial surface ice, known as "the pack," eventually crushed the vessel, leaving the crew with three 22-foot lifeboats, but no ocean to navigate. They trekked toward mainland Antarctica only to find the gap between their locale and destination widening as the pack drifted northward. **40>** **Shackleton, a lifetime explorer, rationalized that two things could destroy survival chances:** starvation and insanity. And he fought vigorously to deny the latter, cognizant of its power. His calmness, self-control and persuasive ability convinced the men their existence depended on each other. **50>** **For 16 months, they survived on rations,** the meat of penguins, seals and sled dogs, and Shackleton's optimistic leadership before finally launching the lifeboats amidst the cracking ice, and reaching the diminutive, deserted Elephant Island. Upon reaching land, Shackleton and five others set sail in a lifeboat for an 800-mile journey through the stormy South Sea toward South Georgia Island, where a whaling village held hope of rescue. **60>** **The makeshift vessel miraculously reached South Georgia Island,** albeit on the wrong side. Three of the six men, Shackleton included, then hiked through the treacherous mountain terrain, avoiding deep crevasses that dared a misstep, before finally reaching the same village they had left 17 months earlier. But the pack now trapped Elephant Island, delaying a final rescue for four more months. **70>** **Teamwork, perseverance, optimism, luck, leadership and the ability to adapt** kept all 28 men alive. That lesson was not lost on the football players who sat in the Feinstein IMAX Theatre that day.

BILL BELICHICK
TAUGHT HIS TEAM
A LESSON ON
OVERCOMING
ADVERSITY

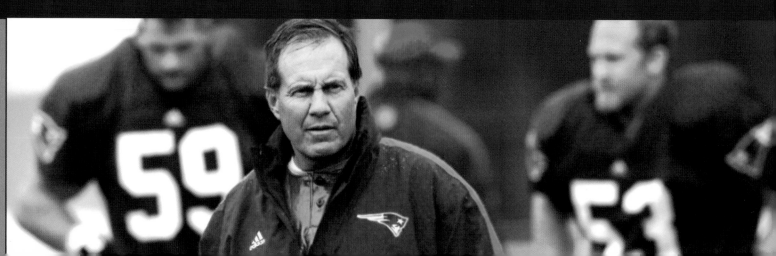

Week One of training camp featured enough other oddities to fill one of those bloated playbooks, and left pretentious prognosticators presuming the worst for a club recovering from a 5-11 season and seemingly spiraling further downward. The chaos caused *Boston Herald* columnist Steve Buckley to opine, "The more things change, the more they remain the same. No matter how splendidly things seem to be going, no matter how placid the Foxboro or Smithfield, R.I., waters may be, there is always some new calamity, some new Chaplinesque pratfall, waiting in the wings."

Such was the mentality created by the Patriots of yore. Nevertheless, it was an accurate depiction of camp's kickoff.

Guard Joe Panos, another free agent expected to vie for a starting assignment on the offensive line, shocked the camp by announcing his retirement, after successfully completing the conditioning test.

And then there was Andy (AWOL) Katzenmoyer. The Patriots linebacker, set to return from neck surgery, appeared at breakfast before the official first full-squad, full-pads practice, but then disappeared without a trace.

These developments had Belichick scratching his head in wonderment. "We're looking for Andy Katzenmoyer," the perplexed coach explained. "I don't know where he is. I mean, my sense is that he left; I don't think he was kidnapped, but I don't know."

Wide receiver Terry Glenn returned after off-season troubles stemming from a spring arrest sent him into typical Terry seclusion. His problems were only beginning. Free agent running back hopeful Antowain Smith reported to Smithfield out of shape and failed his conditioning test – an inauspicious start to his Patriots career that left early camp competition to J.R. Redmond, Kevin Faulk and rookie Walter Williams.

Panos, conversely, notified Belichick of his decision, but it came as no less of a surprise than Katzenmoyer's disappearance.

"If he's going to make that decision," quarterback Drew Bledsoe said, "guard is not a position where you can come in and fake it. If he wasn't ready to go, then he made the right decision. I respect that, and I think everybody does. You can't come in and play this game if your heart's not in it and you're [not] ready to go."

61

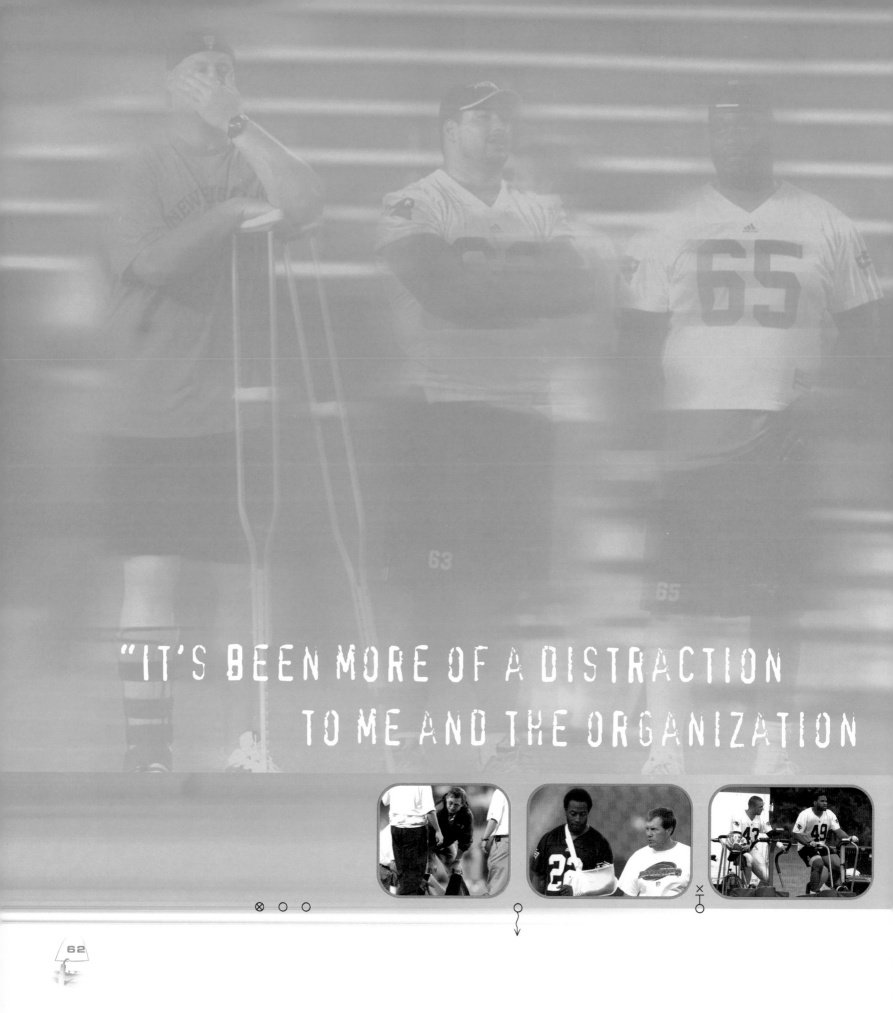

"IT'S BEEN MORE OF A DISTRACTION TO ME AND THE ORGANIZATION

ABOVE AT ONE POINT IN CAMP, THE ENTIRE PROJECTED STARTING OFFENSIVE LINE WAS OUT WITH INJURIES LEFT TO RIGHT HEAD TRAINE

Additionally, cornerback Terrance Shaw, guard Joe Andruzzi and Glenn dropped with injuries on Day Two. The next morning tackle Matt Light went down. Within 24 hours, guard Mike Compton and Bledsoe joined the injury parade. And on Day Six, center Damien Woody hobbled off the field – the same morning that news broke of Minnesota tackle Korey Stringer's heat stroke-induced death, which left the league pondering prevention issues and searching for answers a day too late.

Before the first week closed, tackle Adrian Klemm dislocated his elbow, sidelining all five projected offensive line starters and adding to a pre-camp injury list that included defensive linemen Willie McGinest and Brandon Mitchell. Despair never entered the locker room, even as an offensive line desperately seeking cohesion realized the only thing it had in common was the injury list. The walking wounded resurrected nightmares of Belichick's first Patriots training camp when a scheduled scrimmage with the Giants was cancelled because New England lacked healthy bodies up front.

Belichick would have been forgiven if he had crawled into the training room begging for migraine-relieving medication.

His leadership-by-example and uncanny ability to continue moving forward because "we have to" kept his team focused on each day's considerable workload. He remained positive, noting that none of the injuries was serious in nature and then continued to improve his football team by signing linebacker Bryan Cox on July 31.

But that whirlwind week left *Patriots Football Weekly* to ponder, "It can't get worse from here on in, can it?"

The answer, unfortunately, was an emphatic yes.

The second week started innocently with linebacker Roman Phifer joining the club, but his August 3 arrival coincided with Glenn's dubious escape. Glenn, a.k.a The Distraction, was suspended for four games by the NFL for violating its substance abuse policy, and unwilling to shoulder any blame, he pointed fingers at the Patriots and the league before saddling up and riding out of town unannounced.

Throughout the camp soap opera, Belichick refused to let any one player disrupt his training camp and even left every available door open for his distraught wide receiver.

"Assuming he comes back and works and makes a commitment to the team, I think there is a place for him," Belichick said. "It's been more of a distraction to me and the organization than the players. Terry hasn't been around that much to be a distraction to them. He was around for a few days in the off-season and for a couple of practices here at training camp. He hasn't been an integral part in anything the team has done since the end of the 2000 season. As far as me, I'd like to be devoting more time to our football team, and this has taken up some of my time and energy."

THAN THE PLAYERS"

- BILL BELICHICK

RON O'NEIL, TERRANCE SHAW AND BILL BELICHICK, JOHNNY MCWILLIAMS AND JABARI HOLLOWAY, WILLIE MCGINEST, ADRIAN KLEMM

A SPECIAL CHAMPIONSHIP CONTRIBUTION

By Bill Belichick, Patriots Head Coach

0> *As the season progressed* and we started stringing together the victories, one of the big themes people attached to the team was the amount of adversity we had overcome. Several times, people asked me questions that went something like, "Bill, how have the players been able to thrive despite so many ordeals that usually ruin seasons?" The questioners always mentioned the same laundry list of problems: injuries to the offensive line, a couple of players disappearing from training camp, a player retiring after the first day of camp, having to fine and later suspend a player, and certain football decisions that received mixed reviews. **1|0>** *One subject always included was the death of our quarterbacks coach,* Dick Rehbein. But for every coach, player and member of our organization – really, anyone who knew Dick Rehbein – this tragedy was not to be lumped in with the rest. Something this heartbreaking occupied its own place in our season and it will always stand alone in our memory as a devastating loss that went above and beyond any ordinary distraction we'd ever experienced. **2|0>** *Dick was an exceedingly kind man who, above all else, cherished his family to an incredible degree.* I know of few men with more love and joy for their wife and children than Dick Rehbein. And I know of few NFL coaches as dedicated to their job, their players and their organization as Dick Rehbein. By themselves, each of these traits is something to be proud of. Somehow, Dick accomplished both. **3|0>** *As for his contributions to our Super Bowl season,* here's the bottom line: Dick didn't attend one meeting during the 2001 season, he wasn't at one practice and he was not physically present for one game during the championship run. **4|0>** *That said, I speak for all our players and coaches* in saying without hesitation... the Patriots would not be Super Bowl champions if not for Dick Rehbein. Here's why. One of our core philosophies is that more important than the will to win is the will to prepare to win. The 2001 Patriots embodied that principle. The players did a tremendous job getting ready to play the games. But that commitment to prepare didn't start the week of Opening Day and it didn't start in training camp, either. It went back to the off-season program in March, the passing camp in May, the mini-camp in June and all the hours of meetings and work that led up to training camp. Nobody was more important to the development of our players, particularly on offense, than Dick. That's a pretty tangible contribution. **5|0>** *I'll speak for everyone again when I say that Dick's spirit lives on* through all of us every single day. That's also a tangible contribution. So while Dick's physical absence continues to bring us great sorrow, what is left to fill the void – and then some – is the force that his presence in spirit brought to our championship along with our appreciation for simply knowing such a decent man. It was a privilege.

QUARTERBACKS COACH DICK REHBEIN WATCHES PRACTICE WITH TOM BRADY AND DREW BLEDSOE

AS IT HAPPENED, THE NEW YORK GIANTS WERE SET TO ARRIVE IN RHODE ISLAND THE NEXT DAY

On August 15, though, the unexcused absences landed Glenn, temporarily at least, on the reserve/left camp list, apparently ending his 2001 season. The resolution of the Glenn fiasco was still months away, and his first of many grievances came two weeks later as he sought a return to active duty.

On August 6, Glenn's defection was deemed unimportant in life's grand scheme when, during a media session with NFL on-field officials, a Patriots staffer interrupted director of media relations Stacey James. James returned baring the devastating news that quarterbacks coach Dick Rehbein, 45, was dead, a victim of cardiomyopathy – a disease of the heart muscle first diagnosed in 1988.

Injuries, failed conditioning tests, immature players and even football bowed its collective head in prayer and mourning for the Rehbein family – wife Pam and daughters Betsy and Sarabeth.

As it happened, the New York Giants, for whom Rehbein worked for eight of his 23 NFL seasons before moving to New England, were set to arrive in Rhode Island the next day. The timing made it possible for his New York friends and colleagues to attend funeral services held near the Bryant College campus. With heavy hearts the teams returned to work for two days of inter-squad practices in preparation for the August 10 pre-season opener at Foxboro Stadium, a 14-0 game which New England dominated.

With campus construction limiting fan attendance to the two-team workouts, the Patriots aired a first-of-its-kind live webcast of the two-day practice sessions, allowing fans to log on to patriots.com and watch live action with color commentary.

65

Meanwhile, the Patriots continued to disregard distractions and combat adversity on their way to dismantling Carolina, 23-8, in their second pre-season tune-up. Reserve quarterback Tom Brady impressed in his bid to scale the depth chart, completing 11-of-18 passes for 122 yards and leading two touchdown drives while garnering playing time with the starting offense.

The Panthers game signaled an end to training camp as the trucks packed up and headed back to Foxboro Stadium for one final season. Two pre-season exhibitions remained, but a sense of relief awaited in the cozy Patriots home locker room as Camp SOS mercifully ended.

Through the fog drifted some answers about the 2001 Patriots. The injury-riddled offensive line, unable to come together during camp, remained an uncertainty, but as healthy bodies returned to the fray, improvement was forthcoming.

After Katzenmoyer's decision to undergo a second straight season-ending surgery, the addition of Cox, Phifer and Mike Vrabel added previously unseen depth and experience at linebacker.

The secondary made strides, thanks to the Shaw and Terrell Buckley signings, along with an improved commitment from Ty Law and better consistency from Tebucky Jones.

Tight end remained an enigma with two drafted rookies – Jabari Holloway and Arther Love – spending all of camp injured and Rod Rutledge and Jermaine Wiggins only able to play limited roles.

Wide receiver David Patten and tackle Matt Light excelled as the camp's biggest surprises and both filled important voids on the offense.

Just as things started to brighten in late August, the Tampa Bay Buccaneers hovered over the Patriots like an ominous cloud. The third pre-season game – generally deemed the most important because starters see the most playing time – delivered a reality check to New England's confidence. Perhaps the unsightly performance was a culmination of adversity finally besting the mentally tired unit. Whatever the subtext, the Patriots were physically pounded on both sides of the ball. It was a 20-3 drubbing by a superior team, leaving all to wonder if these were was the same old soft Patriots, unable to deal with the NFL's tough guys.

A disconsolate Belichick uttered the obvious. "I didn't think it was a very good performance by our football team tonight."

The game represented a step back for a team that tried to overcome more adversity in August than one team ordinarily experiences in an entire season. But it also served as a valuable wake-up call. A week later, New England rebounded to rattle the Washington Redskins, 33-13, in the pre-season finale at Foxboro Stadium.

With the exhibition slate complete, it was on to Cincinnati for Kickoff Weekend and a date with the lowly Bengals. The bell was about to ring on the 2001 season and Belichick was about to find out if he had found his winners.

The jury was out.

LEFT TO RIGHT ANTHONY PLEASANT, TOM BRADY, DEFENSE VS. TAMPA BAY, OTIS SMITH

ABOVE PATRIOTS AND PANTHERS LINE UP FOR THEIR PRE-SEASON TUSSLE

CHAPTER 4

WHEN FOOTBALL GAMES DON'T MATTER

KICKOFF WEEKEND.

THE SACRED BEGINNING TO A FIVE-MONTH

HOLIDAY SEASON CELEBRATED SUNDAY

AFTERNOONS IN A MOST AMERICAN

FASHION. INCREASINGLY, NFL SUNDAY

HAS BECOME A FAMILY AFFAIR, RATHER

THAN THE BOYS CLUB IT ONCE WAS,

AS THE GAME HAS EMERGED INTO

THE NEW NATIONAL PASTIME.

The National Football League is everywhere on NFL Sunday, garnering the kind of coverage that even the World Series fails to obtain. NFL pre-game shows lure viewers to their television sets early Sunday mornings; the football fan's answer to the political junkie's *Meet the Press*, as dominical television staples. The games themselves are "appointment" TV. *Monday Night Football* is an institution.

The NFL has become the ideal combination of sport and entertainment. It is why cars, trucks, vans and RVs typically line Route 1 awaiting the 9 a.m. game day opening of Foxboro Stadium parking lots – the swing of the gate invites passage into the heart of day-long celebration; the tailgate party.

Sausage, steak tips, hamburgers, whole turkeys, beer, tables and chairs, couches, tents, TVs, radios, heaters, generators and grills are arranged in intricate configurations as hundreds of makeshift outdoor living rooms are formed. Thousands of Pats fans socialize, moving from "home" to "home," talking football, life, family and kids with their football friends. The tailgate gathering has become America's block party, an institution of small town socialization in big city stadia. In the Foxboro lots, homemade flagpoles adorned with banners of Patriots colors flapping in the wind are totems to home team pride.

In 2001, one game into the new season, those flagpoles would fly the red-white-and-blue for an altogether different reason.

American President George Bush's league-wide opening day coin toss on September 9, 2001, raised the curtain on the new NFL season. Two days later, Bush stood with and for his country as the unflappable leader of a nation under attack.

America was still enjoying the Good Life before September 11 when Bush appeared on the scoreboard video screen at Cincinnati's Paul Brown Stadium as the Patriots prepared to kick off Year Two of the Bill Belichick era.

The President was ushering in a rite of fall – a moment anticipated by Patriots fans anxious to erase the memories of the previous season. A 3-1 pre-season offered hope, as did Game One's opponent, the lowly Bengals.

The only discordant note in this sea of optimism was that most prognosticators pegged the Patriots for last place in the AFC East. "The Pats signed a bunch of free agents from the NFL five-and-dime store." – *Street & Smith's*, predicting a fifth-place finish. "Coming off a 5-11 season with loads of holes to fill, Belichick tried to cut-and-paste his way back to respectability with cheap free agents." – *Athlon*, also pegging the Pats for fifth.

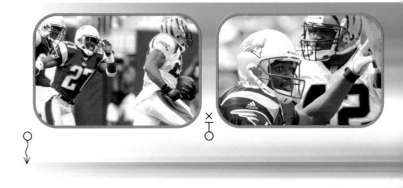

Despite widespread media pessimism, Patriots players sensed a revival. "I think this team has come a long way since the first day of training camp," tight end Jermaine Wiggins told the *Boston Globe*. "We've really come together as a team."

The team's fortitude was tested early in camp and again as the season neared. A Terry Glenn grievance hearing – one that would eventually lead to reinstatement of the oft-troubled receiver – interrupted preparation for Week One. But Belichick kept his team focused. While Glenn and news of long-time Patriot Gino Cappelletti's open-heart surgery spawned

LEFT TO RIGHT BENGALS COREY DILLON, TROY BROWN, DREW BLEDSOE

headlines, a minor detail that would have a far greater impact in 2001 was developing.

Belichick's September 4 announcement that Tom Brady had leap-frogged Damon Huard to number two on the quarterback depth chart was hardly shocking to anyone who had watched the second-year passer throughout training camp. "Based on the pre-season, we just feel like Tom right now is a little bit ahead of Damon in terms of handling the team," Belichick explained. "Tom has a lot of natural leadership."

With the durable Drew Bledsoe entrenched as the franchise quarterback, naming the back-up didn't exactly send the Richter scale into a frenzy.

A lackluster 23-17 opening week loss to the Bengals did, however, send tremors throughout New England and seemed to confirm the region's worst fears. The nightmarish perform-ance rekindled bad memories of 2000. The offense stumbled behind a non-existent ground game and a relatively ineffective passing attack. The defense was ripped apart for big plays, and special teams offered no refuge.

71

By Joe Andruzzi, Patriots offensive lineman

0> *One of my three brothers* told me after the Super Bowl that it was destiny for us. The Patriots. The red-white-and-blue. It was supposed to happen that way in a year like we had, the nation had. We played together as a team and showed our unity as a team, as a nation. It ended up being perfect. **10>** **But the September 11 tragedy** was obviously a stressful time in the lives of a lot of people, and especially mine and my family's. I was sitting in a dentist chair when I heard the news on the radio. They said a small plane hit the World Trade Center and I thought it was just an accident. I later turned on the radio in my car and found out it was a bigger plane and that everyone was going crazy. I was listening to Howard Stern, who is based in New York, and he jokes around all the time, but he was suddenly very serious. I picked up my wife, Jennifer, and my kids, Hunter and Breanna, and we went home and sat in front of the TV. It didn't take long for the shock to set in. **20>** **I had a feeling** that at least one, if not all three of my brothers who are New York firefighters, were down there and we couldn't get a hold of anyone in my family for the longest time. I called everyone I knew and usually got a busy signal or a tornado-warning message. Finally, about five hours later, my dad called. My brother, Jimmy, had given his phone number to a stranger on the street and the stranger called my parents and said, "Your son is O.K." **30>** **It was pretty rough on everybody.** It was excruciating not knowing if my brothers were safe and then finding out they were all O.K. But they're not really O.K. There were a lot of people I knew down there. My brothers knew personally more than 200 of the 350 firefighters who were lost. We almost lost Jimmy who escaped the second tower literally seconds before it collapsed. **40>** **We're a close Italian family** and this has brought us even closer, and I think a lot of families became closer that week. That is why it was important for the NFL to cancel the games that week. It was a time to be with family and loved ones. I know I couldn't have focused on my work. **50>** **When we returned on September 23** for the Jets game, it was a pretty emotional day. My brothers were exhausted from working 24 hours-on, 24 hours-off down at Ground Zero, as it now was called. They came up to Foxboro for that game and partook in the pre-game ceremonies and a ceremonial coin toss. They didn't come for themselves or me, but for the whole nation. They wore their Fire Department of New York outfits because they were representing those 350 heroes who gave their lives. It felt a little different hearing the fans cheer for them, because as a football player, I'm used to hearing them cheer for us. The fans said thank you in a special way. **60>** **I just want to remind everyone** that Family comes first. When you dig down deep and need to think and talk about the real stuff, it's your family and loved ones who are there for you. September 11 was just another reminder of that.

The family of guard Joe Andruzzi was saluted as honorary captains for the September 23 game against the Jets. Bill Andruzzi, a retired New York City police officer, was joined by three of his sons, Billy, Jimmy and Marc – all New York firefighters who answered the call during the attack at the World Trade Center towers on September 11. "It is an honor to recognize the Andruzzi family," Patriots owner Bob Kraft said. "They represent many of the real American heroes. We salute the Andruzzis and the many brave men and women like them who have been willing to risk their

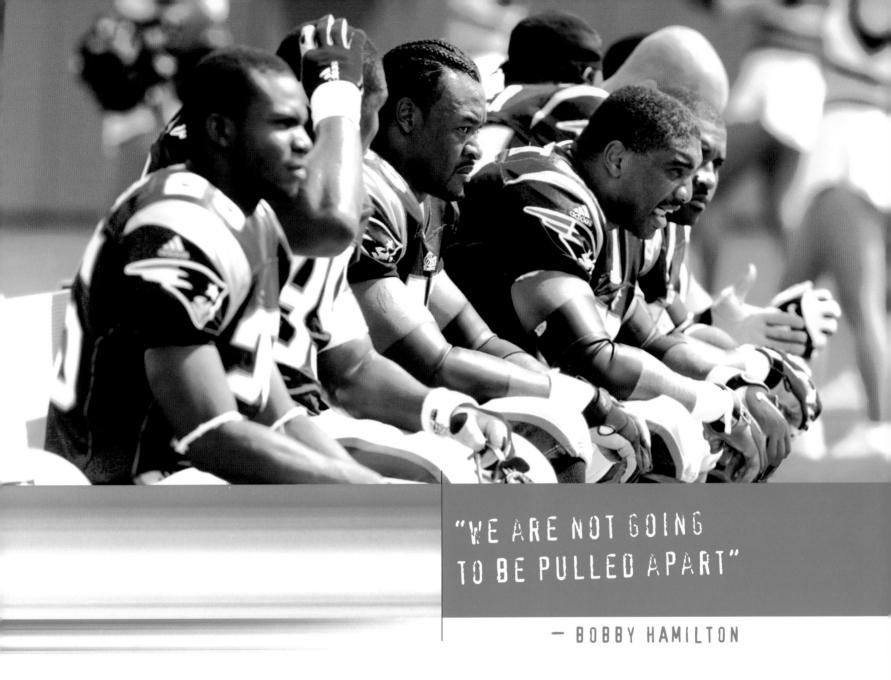

"WE ARE NOT GOING TO BE PULLED APART"

— BOBBY HAMILTON

Same old story. The Cincinnati game unfolded like so many in Belichick's first year; a third-quarter swoon capped by a fourth-quarter comeback bid falling short. Bledsoe also fell short on his own with a controversial decision late in the game to audible to a quarterback sneak on fourth-and-two. He was stopped an inch shy of the first down marker. Bengals ball. Game over.

Defensive lineman Bobby Hamilton's post-game clubhouse howl summarized the moment's emotion. "We can't let this happen again," he told *Boston Globe* columnist Michael Holley.

"We have too many guys in this room who won't let last year happen again." But in the wake of an 0-1 start, it appeared nothing had changed for a team still more than willing to suffer lengthy mental lapses and lethargy during games.

"Nobody is going to let any negativism about the team come in [to this locker room]. We'll seal it off. We're not going to be pulled apart," Hamilton added.

Neither would the country be torn asunder. Two days later, the nation collectively locked arms and essentially echoed Hamilton's words in a show of unity and true patriotism in the wake of an unspeakable tragedy.

73

That's when four commercial airliners bound for transcontinental trips to California, two of which originated from Boston's Logan International Airport, were hijacked. The Boston planes, United Airlines Flight 175 and American Airlines Flight 11, plunged into the sides of New York's World Trade Center twin towers. A third plane crashed into the Pentagon in Washington D.C., with a fourth meeting a fiery end in a field outside Pittsburgh. The 108-story twin towers – the tallest skyscrapers in the city – eventually collapsed from the intense heat of the fires, burying civilians and leaving mounds of rubble eight stories high, providing a focal point for American angst, and resolve.

The continental United States was attacked in a ferocious act of terrorism, leaving thousands dead and a shocked nation in mourning and seeking justice. President Bush acted swiftly and strongly in response to the aggression.

"Tonight we are a country awakened to danger and called to defend freedom. Our grief has turned to anger, and anger to resolution. Whether we bring our enemies to justice, or bring justice to our enemies, justice will be done," he said in a speech to a joint session of Congress.

The tragedy struck close to home for the Patriots. Guard Joe Andruzzi's three brothers – Billy, Jim and Marc are New York City firefighters and were called to the Lower Manhattan scene. Jim Andruzzi was among the first 500 firefighters to arrive and he escaped scant seconds before the second tower collapsed.

"The hardest part was trying to find out where they were," a tearful Joe said in the wake of the catastrophe. "One of my brothers was in the building. He got out just in time."

Within 48 hours, NFL commissioner Paul Tagliabue announced the postponement of the league's Week Two games, noting the need to recover and pay respect to the families and loved ones of those perished.

"We in the National Football League have decided that our priorities for this weekend are to pause, grieve and reflect. It's a time to tend to families and neighbors and all those wounded by these horrific acts of terrorism. We understand those individuals in sports who want to play this weekend. We also can empathize with those who want to take the weekend off and resume their personal lives and professional careers next week. We strongly believe that the latter course of action is the right decision for the NFL," Tagliabue said. "On Sunday, September 23, the NFL, its players and coaches will return stronger than ever and resume our playing schedule."

"WE IN THE NFL

HAVE DECIDED THAT OUR PRIORITIES
FOR THIS WEEKEND ARE TO PAUSE,
GRIEVE AND REFLECT"

— NFL COMMISSIONER, PAUL TAGLIABUE

— BILLY, JIM AND MARC ARE
CALLED TO THE LOWER MANHATTAN SCENE

A CHANGING LANDSCAPE

0> *Freedom and normalcy* were redefined on September 11, 2001. **1 0>** *The horrific terrorist attack on America* sent shockwaves through all aspects of life. Football crowds milled outside stadium entrances long before game time simply to avoid missing the opening kickoff. Paying customers who long had enjoyed Patriots football despite Foxboro Stadium's uncomfortable metal benches waited inordinate amounts of time for yellow-jacketed stadium security personnel to frisk each entrant, turning away those with bags no longer permitted through the gate. Patriots employees who generally flashed a pass and waltzed to work faced a security check and a bag search. It was the same for the media – a rummage through the workbag and a quick pat down even for writers who had trudged up to the stadium press box for all 31 years of its existence. **2 0>** *And nobody said a word.* Nobody complained when the number of uniformed police officers present increased tenfold, giving an appearance of insecurity more than its converse. **3 0>** *Call it new freedom,* which may be the polite term for less freedom. Call it new normalcy, which may be the diplomatic classification for abnormal. In this sense the terrorists won. They hurt us emotionally and exposed our vulnerability. They instilled fear in our lives. **4 0>** *But in doing so,* they strengthened our senses and our resolve. They didn't stop us from living. Football fans showed up in droves at NFL stadiums on September 23 without fear. They showed up decorated in red, white and blue, chanting U-S-A, draped in Old Glory and with the Stars and Stripes painted on their faces. They delivered the message that you can knock America down, but never out. **5 0>** *The terrorists changed our lives forever,* no question, but we responded with greater intensity, renewed purpose and steeled will. Our leaders urged us to return to our normal lives. So we did even without knowing if it was possible. And we did it as one with our freedom intact. Terrorism didn't defeat America. It strengthened it. **6 0>** *It took longer to get into a football game* after September 11. So what? We still came by the thousands and the players played, just as before.

THE SEPTEMBER 23 GAME AT FOXBORO STADIUM SAW AN INCREASED SENSE OF PATRIOTISM AND LONGER LINES DUE TO INCREASED SECURITY MEASURES

UNITED WE STOOD. UNITED WE STAND. STILL

Critics of the commissioner's decision, a minuscule minority, argued that to allow a disruption was admitting defeat, giving the terrorists what they sought. They called for immediate return to normalcy – a word newly defined after a vulnerable nation saw a sliver of its freedom sliced away. Yet the players, almost to a man, applauded the postponement. "You have to look at the typical response of our culture," linebacker Ted Johnson said. "Sweep it under the rug and move on. Pretend it didn't happen. This is real-life stuff. Our nation needs to grieve. It needs to assess what happened. To bury our feelings and say life goes on – that's not appropriate."

The schedule was altered when the NFL reached an agreement with the National Automobile Dealers Association to move its New Orleans convention up one week.

That enabled the Super Bowl to be pushed back to February 3 from January 27 and the Week Two games to be added to the end of the NFL's original schedule without affecting the 12-team playoff format.

When games resumed on September 23, American patriotism was alive and well. American flags flew from cars, homes and businesses. A group of terrorists looking to break America only awakened and strengthened her.

Suddenly, it was honorable to wear the Patriots red, white and blue as if New England's players represented the freedom and independence threatened on September 11, 2001 – a date never to be forgotten, with victims who shall always be remembered.

United We Stood. United We Stand. Still.

83

September 11th 2001

American Airlines Flight 11

Barbara Arestegui
Jeffrey Collman
Sara Low
Karen Martin
Thomas McGuinness
Betty Ong
Kathleen Nicosia
Jean Roger

Dianne Snyder
Madeline Sweeney
Anna Williams Allison
David Angell
Lynn Angell
Seima Aoyama
Christine Barbuto
Berry Berenson
Carolyn Beug
Carol Bouchard
Robin Caplin

Neilie Casey
Jeffrey Coombs
Tara Creamer
Thelma Cuccinello

Pentagon

Spc. Craig Amundson
Melissa Rose Barnes
Sgt. Max Beilke
Ada R. Bishundat
Carrie Blagburn
Lisa Garfield Boone
Donna Gowen
Sharon Boyle
Christopher L. Burford
H. Caballero

NYPD

Sgt. John Coughlin
Sgt. Michael Curtin
Sgt. Rodney Gillis
Sgt. Timothy Roy
Dt. Claude Richards
Dt. Joseph Vigiano
John D'Allara

FDNY

Brian Ahearn
Eric Allen
Richard Allen
James Amato
Joseph Amatuccia
Christopher Amoroso
Calixto Anaya Jr
Jean Andrucki
Joseph Angelini
Joseph Angelini Jr
Faustino Apostol
David Arce
Louis Arena
Richard Aronow
Carl Asaro
Gregg Atlas

United Airlines Flight 175

THE SEPTEMBER 11 TRAGEDY CARRIED OVER TO SUPER BOWL XXXVI WHERE PRE-GAME AND HALF-TIME CEREMONIES MEMORIALIZED THOSE LOST

CHAPTER 5

DOUBTING THOMAS

SAN MATEO IS A BUSTLING

NORTHERN CALIFORNIA CITY NESTLED

ON THE BANKS OF SAN FRANCISCO BAY.

MORE THAN 93,000 INHABITANTS

LIVE WITHIN THIS AFFLUENT URBAN

CONGLOMERATION IN A 14-SQUARE-MILE

AREA FRAMED BY A SCENIC COASTLINE

AND MAGNIFICENT REDWOODS.

TOM BRADY GREW UP
IDOLIZING HIS LOCAL
NFL HERO:

49ERS HALL OF FAME QUARTERBACK

ABOVE JOE MONTANA **LEFT TO RIGHT** TOM BRADY'S CLOSE-KNIT FAMILY HAS BEEN A BIG PART OF HIS FOOTBALL CAREER FROM HIS DAYS AT JUNIPERO SERRA HIGH SCHOOL TO THE UNIVERSITY OF MICHIGAN AND TO THE PATRIOTS, WHERE THE SECOND-YEAR PRO BLOSSOMED INTO A POISED TEAM LEADER AND SUPER BOWL MVP QUARTERBACK

The town, incorporated in 1894, is the birthplace and home of Tom Brady. The youngest of four children and the only boy, Tom grew up idolizing his local NFL hero, 49ers Hall of Fame quarterback Joe Montana.

The slender, but athletic Brady evolved from a sandlot denizen into a clutch two-sport star at Junipero Serra High School in San Mateo – a boys-only Catholic institution of fewer than one 1,000 students and the alma mater of NFL Hall of Fame wide receiver Lynn Swann and Major League superstar Barry Bonds.

Brady, who didn't even begin playing schoolboy football until a junior, earned two letters each in baseball and football. Excelling in two sports came easily for the graceful kid blessed with natural ability and a work ethic to match. He soon was asked to choose one for his future. The Montreal Expos drafted the high school catcher in the 18th round of the Major League Baseball Amateur Draft while recruiters from Michigan, Cal-Berkeley, UCLA, USC and Illinois chased the prep All-American quarterback.

He chose college football and Michigan, where he would play in front of six-figure crowds clad in maize-and-blue on Saturday afternoons. No Class A baseball, rickety buses and fast food diets for him.

Once in Ann Arbor, however, the blue chip recruit found himself entangled in a five-year struggle to secure precious playing time, which he fought and scratched for until the day he rallied the Wolverines from a 14-point deficit in an Orange Bowl victory over Alabama to complete his collegiate career.

Despite completing 62 percent of his passes for 5,351 yards while compiling a 20-5 record at Michigan, Brady's inability to nail down the full-time starting gig seriously devalued his NFL draft stock, and the Patriots landed him in the sixth round of the 2000 draft with the 199th selection. Motivated by the slight, Brady sought to prove his worth. After a rookie season buried at the bottom of the depth chart, he spent his first professional off-season training physically and mentally to vie for playing time.

The work paid lucrative dividends, but it was his leadership that caught Bill Belichick's eye.

"Tom has a real good personality for a quarterback," the head coach said before Brady's first start. "He is confident, but he is not cocky. He is assertive, but he is not overbearing. He can come on pretty strong and make a point or get a point across without being antagonistic or offensive in doing it."

In his second professional training camp, Brady overtook Michael Bishop and Damon Huard to seize the back-up quarterback role while nipping at the heels of eight-year starter and three-time Pro Bowler, Drew Bledsoe, the franchise quarterback with a new multi-year, multimillion-dollar contract.

JOE MONTANA

THE STANDING OVATION THAT GREETED THE QUARTET WAS BOTH HEARTFELT AND A BALM

Fate would conspire to seal the future of the quarterbacking tandem during a most emotional time for all. Patriots Nation and the NFL were picking up the pieces when the league resumed its playing schedule on September 23, two weeks after the calamitous events of 9-11. The New York Jets apprehensively boarded an airplane, leaving their hometown devastation en route to Foxboro Stadium for an emotional return to football. With the nation still grieving, the NFL provided needed entertainment and gathering places for Americans to display their pride and spirit, which they did league-wide in heart-wrenching pre-game ceremonies honoring the heroes in New York, Washington D.C., and those aboard the ill-fated flight that crashed in Pennsylvania.

The Patriots extended their gratitude to offensive guard Joe Andruzzi's family during a spirited observance of pride and unity. The standing ovation from the 60,292 in attendance that greeted the quartet was both heartfelt and a balm. "It was a great honor for them," Joe said after the game. "I was happy to see everyone recognize them as the [real] heroes."

ABOVE THE ANDRUZZIS HAD MORE THAN MOST TO BE THANKFUL FOR AND TO MOURN AFTER SEPTEMBER 11

Perhaps it was the hangover effect from an emotional two weeks, but neither the Jets nor Patriots looked particularly crisp in New York's 10-3 win.

Four Patriots turnovers in the game, including a Bledsoe interception in the end zone and a Marc Edwards fumble on the Jets 7-yard line, undermined New England's chances. New York's Curtis Martin pranced, danced and barreled his way for 106 yards on 24 carries and the game's only touchdown.

And then, with 5:11 remaining on the Foxboro Stadium game clock, the Patriots season and future changed forever. While trying to scramble outside the pocket for a first down, Bledsoe was met with a jarring, high-velocity, head-on blow from Jets linebacker Mo Lewis along the Patriots sideline. The bone-crushing impact knocked the quarterback to the ground where he lay motionless for long moments until he was helped up. He passed sideline concussion tests and actually played one more series before Belichick lifted him from the game.

The initial diagnosis of Bledsoe's injury hardly caused panic or even concern. But 45 minutes after the game, doctors discovered internal injuries and rushed Bledsoe to Massachusetts General Hospital by ambulance, where blood was drained from his chest – the result of a sheared blood vessel.

ABOVE A HAIL MARY FALLS TO THE GROUND AGAINST THE N.Y. JETS AS THE PATRIOTS FALL TO 0-2 LEFT TO RIGHT THE JETS JAMES FARRIOR, TROY BROWN, MARC EDWARDS

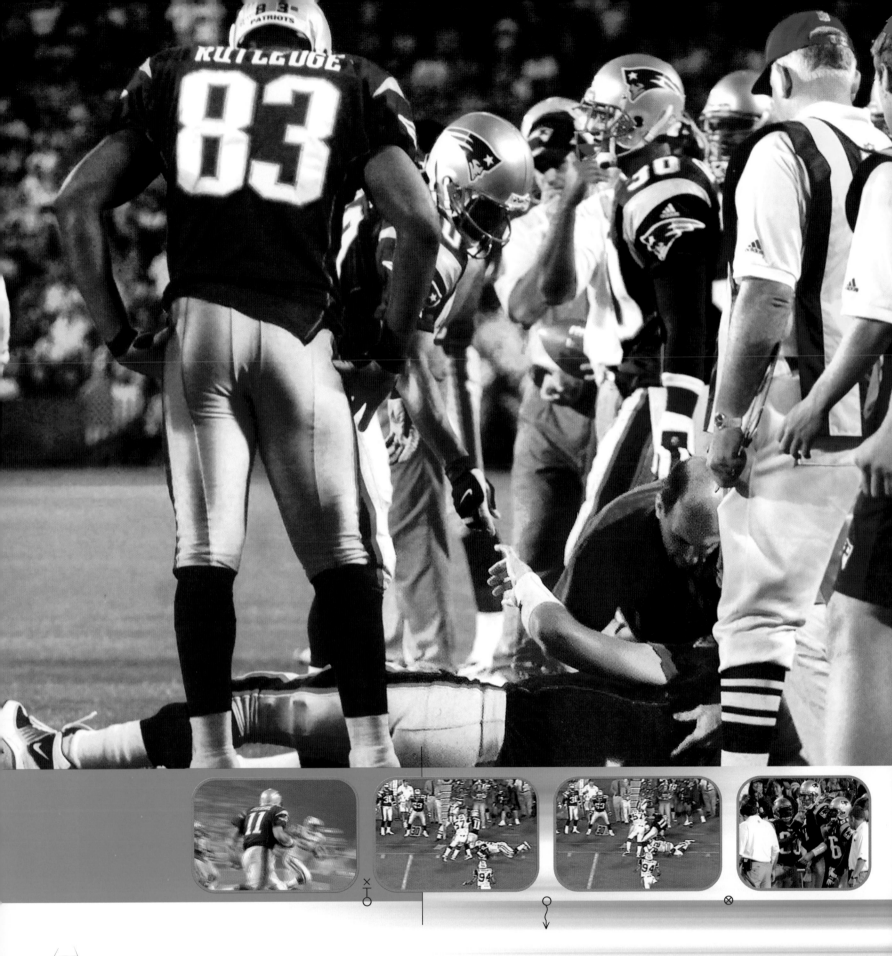

ABOVE THE HIT THAT CHANGED A SEASON. MO LEWIS LAYS INTO DREW BLEDSOE, THUS ALTERING THE PATRIOTS FOREVER

"It's some type of internal injury," Belichick said the day after the game, "which isn't what it appeared at the time of the play. Initially it seemed that he had been knocked out for a second. Then after the game it became apparent that this wasn't the issue."

The injury, which could have ended Bledsoe's season, side-lined him indefinitely, and placed New England's hopes on the arm of the untested second-year quarterback from San Mateo. Patriots supporters could not be blamed for tiptoeing toward the life rafts. The team's leaders recognized that mere talk would do them no good.

Bryan Cox's reputation preceded his arrival in New England and the outspoken veteran grabbed center stage as his team prepared for the high-powered Colts. "They can be beat," Cox emphasized. "They put their pants on just like we put our pants on. We can compete. We can play. We can win. I'm looking to knock [Colts quarterback Peyton Manning's] head off. That's point-blank football. You can make them out to be Supermen. You can give them some credit; they've put up a lot of points this season. But I'm not built like that."

"THEY PUT THEIR PANTS ON JUST LIKE WE PUT OUR PANTS ON. WE CAN COMPETE. WE CAN PLAY.

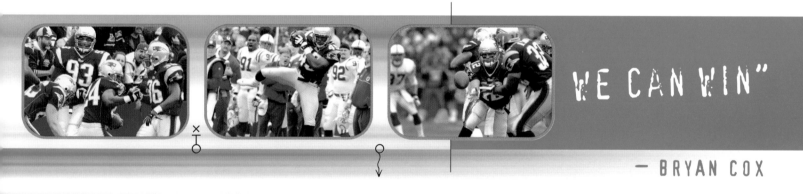

WE CAN WIN"

— BRYAN COX

"We kept saying [last year] we were better than what we were," safety Lawyer Milloy said, "and all of sudden we were at the end of the season and we had five wins."

With no Bledsoe, no signs of encouragement, an 0-2 record and 2-0 Indianapolis coming to town with the league's highest scoring offense, many a meaningless game loomed and the fabled New England foliage had yet to turn.

His words reverberated through the locker room and delivered a forceful message to his teammates. The Colts received that same message a couple days later. Brady's first professional start proved easy and stress-free. His teammates applied the pressure to Manning, as the defense sparked a dominating 44-13 Patriots win.

93

Some seasons have defining moments, a single play that alters the team's errant course, a tipped pass, a fumble, or a kick bouncing off an upright. After two uninspired efforts to start the season, New England was desperate for such a boost. It came in the first quarter of the conquest of Indianapolis, when diminutive Colts wide receiver Jerome Pathon darted through traffic on a crossing pattern. Cox rewarded Pathon's boldness with a hammering jolt, planting him into the turf and then standing over him like a feral beast about to feast on his prey, while keeping scavengers at bay.

The hit awakened a slumbering Patriots team that suddenly seemed a step quicker, as its aroused defense swarmed the big three of Manning, running back Edgerrin James and wide receiver Marvin Harrison.

The opportunistic defense intercepted Manning three times, including touchdown returns of 78 and 23 yards. The Colts Pro Bowl passer was bewildered by Belichick's defensive scheme and remained a winless 0-4 in Foxboro Stadium. The Patriots physical defensive play proved contagious, as an unproven Patriots offensive line blew Colts defenders off the ball all game long.

COX REWARDED PATHON'S BOLDNESS WITH A HAMMERING JOLT, PLANTING HIM INTO THE TURF

ABOVE LEFT   BRYAN COX HOVERS OVER INDY'S JEROME PATHON AFTER HIS MOMENTUM-CHANGING TACKLE

LEFT TO RIGHT   TEDY BRUSCHI, ROMAN PHIFER, ANTOWAIN SMITH

New England finished with 177 rushing yards, 94 from Antowain Smith, who contributed two rushing touchdowns.

In his first start, a conservative Brady finished a modest 13-of-23 for 168 yards with no touchdowns or interceptions. Nothing more was required, but there was no hint of future greatness, either.

New England's convincing win with Brady at the helm somehow restored hope. But as the team boarded its Northwest Airlines charter bound for Miami and an October 7 date with the Dolphins, a trip to South Florida's heat was sure to provide a stiffer test, and the meltdown that ensued raised red danger flags about the future.

Add star return specialist Troy Brown's fumble inside the Patriots 5-yard line and the result was one of the worst blowouts in Belichick's stint as head coach, 30-10.

"We just got our butts kicked today," Belichick said. "We just didn't play as well as they did, not even close. They were a better football team in every phase of the game."

Change was obviously necessary with a 1-3 record threatening to choke the air from another Patriots season. That's when Brady discreetly approached Milloy to discuss the team's practice habits. The Patriots defensive leader suggested the young quarterback speak his mind to the team.

Minus the emotion present in the Colts win, the defense wilted in Miami. It was torn apart by Dolphins running back Lamar Smith, who whisked through gaping holes for 29 carries, 144 yards and a touchdown. Miami's defense feasted on the Patriots young, inexperienced passer starting his first road game. Brady completed only 12-of-24 passes for an inconsequential 86 yards and his second-half fumble resulted in a Jason Taylor touchdown that extended the Dolphins lead.

"You can't go out and practice average on Wednesday, average on Thursday, okay on Friday and then expect to play well on Sunday," Brady said in a clear message to his teammates. "If you practice great [on those days] there is no reason why you wouldn't come out on Sunday and play great. We're going to start practicing great every day. So there will be no reason to come out on a day like this and play this poorly."

AN HONORABLE LEDGER

By Ron Hobson, *The Patriot Ledger*

0> **In 14 years as a member of the New England Patriots, Bruce Armstrong** saw the best and worst of times. He saw 1-15 and an AFC Championship, and on September 30, 2001 he stood proudly on the Foxboro Stadium turf to be honored for his standout career during half-time of the Patriots first win of the season – a 44-13 thrashing of the Indianapolis Colts. **10>** **The five-year waiting period** was waived for Armstrong to enter the team's Hall of Fame and the respected warrior was voted in on his first try. Neither Armstrong nor anyone else in the old stadium could know that the coming months would be the greatest of times for the Patriots franchise. **20>** **While Armstrong never held the Lombardi Trophy,** he has no complaints after a distinguished career. When he walked away, he had played more games as a Patriot than anyone before him. **30>** **"Somebody called it a meaningless record** and maybe to them it was," the six-time Pro Bowl tackle said. "But it meant everything to me because if you go by the idea that football players play football, then it means that I was a football player for a long time." **40>** **Armstrong was all football player,** starting from Day One as a rookie out of Louisville, first at right tackle and eventually on the left side – the quarterback's blind side. **50>** **He suffered and played** through a number of major injuries during his career but none was as serious as that day in 1992 in Buffalo's Rich Stadium when he and defensive end Bruce Smith got tangled up and Armstrong's knee popped. "He's all done," was the first word that reached the press box soon after the injury. **60>** **Everyone believed it was over** because 300-pounders don't recover easily from major reconstructive knee surgery. Yet Armstrong willed himself back onto the field the following season. He dismisses that injury and all the others sustained over the years as just part of being a left tackle in the NFL. **70>** **"I had four reconstructions,** both knees and both shoulders," Armstrong said, matter-of-factly. "There are other guys that get scoped and cleaned out. I'm not a doctor and don't pretend to be, but if you get scoped and are out playing three days later, then you could have foregone that procedure. Just put a little ice on it and get out there. That's the way I felt about it." **80>** **Besides being physically tough,** Armstrong also was a tough critic as a team leader. He was candid and might have stepped on a few toes while speaking his mind to a teammate or even a coach. But the bonds Armstrong made in his 14 years were strong and he has no regrets. **90>** **"I kind of like where I am,"** said Armstrong. "We all went to college. If someone comes up to you and says, 'OK you do this and at 35 you have X amount of money in the bank and you will be able to play golf for the rest of your life,' what would you do? It's been good and now it's over." **100>** **It may be over,** but it was a heck of a ride.

BRUCE ARMSTRONG WAS A ROCK FOR NEW ENGLAND OVER HIS ENTIRE CAREER AND ON SEPTEMBER 30 BECAME THE EIGHTH PATRIOT TO HAVE HIS NUMBER RETIRED

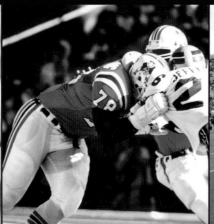

BRADY EMERGED AS A CONFIDENT,

CHARISMATIC COMMANDER

The Patriots seesaw season was teetering on disaster. Its margin for error gone, an indifferent team needed an offensive leader to rally behind, and Brady became that leader. Shielding himself from the horde of doubters, he emerged as a confident, charismatic commander.

"That type of leadership from a guy who just came off the bench and was able to come in and make things happen is rare in a young quarterback," wide receiver Troy Brown said, "but with Tom's energy and enthusiasm, he couldn't keep his mouth shut and that's what we needed. The thing that maybe helped him the most is that we had a bunch of guys in the huddle willing to check their egos at the door and allow a younger guy to do the talking and lead the team the way he did.

"Our offense needed a guy who could go and motivate people even when they really didn't want to be out there. You'd see Tom getting pretty enthusiastic or getting angry with the way guys were practicing sometimes. If you needed somebody pushing you, he was the guy to do it. He'd tell you if you were slacking off. He got everybody fired up in the huddle. I think it excites everyone when you see the quarterback doing those types of things."

While New England's febrile football fans may have been a legion of Doubting Thomases, within the Patriots locker room there was no doubting this Thomas. Brady's leadership, minimized by his critics, helped turn around the season.

FLEET FAN OF THE YEAR

WITHOUT FANS, THERE'S NO PRO FOOTBAL

THE JOSEPH R. MASTRANGELO MEMORIAL TROPHY. IN 1995 FLEET BANK (THEN THE BANK OF BOSTO

1	2	3	4		5
	6	7		9	
			8		
10	11	12	13		14

1 RANDY PIERCE (2001)   2 DAVID BROOKS (2000)   3 MIKE SCHUSTER (1999)   4 CLINT MILLS (199

9 RICHARD PECK (1993)   10 WILL WARNER (1992)   11 BOB MEYERS (1990)   12 DIANE CASSERIN

INCE 1987, THE NEW ENGLAND PATRIOTS HAVE GIVEN OUT ITS FAN OF THE YEAR AWARD. THE WINNER RECEIVES

ECAME THE OFFICIAL SPONSOR OF THE AWARD. PICTURED BELOW ARE ALL THE AWARD'S RECIPIENTS.

ALICE CATALDO (1997)   6 MARK FEIGENBAUM (1996)   7 JIM CAMPBELL (1995)   8 ELAINE TRUDEL (1994)

1989)   13 JACK MCCARTHY (1988)   14 BILL LEONARD (1987)   NOT SHOWN CLINTON COOLIDGE (1991)

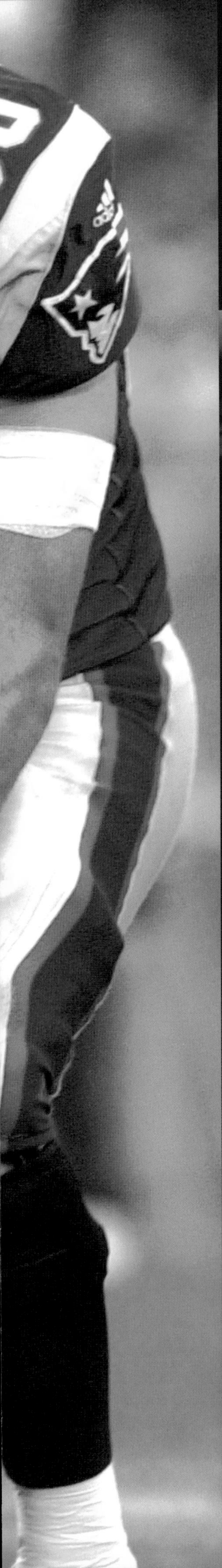

CHAPTER 6

A TEAM EMERGES

THE NFL SEASON IS A POUNDING,

GUT-WRENCHING 16-MILE RACE,

EACH ENSUING MILE MORE IMPORTANT

AND MORE GRUELING THAN THE ONE

BEFORE – NOVEMBER MORE MEANINGFUL

THAN OCTOBER AND DECEMBER EVEN

MORE SO THAN NOVEMBER.

It may appear a marathon in its entirety, but it's actually a series of cumulative sprints – a Tour de France set-up and mentality. Keep the yellow jersey in sight and hope survives. Lose it, and you play for pride.

The 2001 Patriots, an unimpressive 1-3, reached the first turn near the back of the *peloton*. A depressed New England region watched helplessly and angrily as it questioned Bill Belichick – his vaunted defense vulnerable to the run, his offense barely producing. It seemed the post-Super Bowl XXXI decline was destined to continue. That yellow jersey was pulling out of sight somewhere up the road.

All the veterans – those leaders with character added in the off-season – were supposed to alter the course, restore winning ways. It wasn't happening and it appeared to many that it might never happen. Adversity is a given in sports, and the training camp troubles coupled with Drew Bledsoe's chest injury weighed on the team like the anchor that sat in the Patriots locker room – a not-so-subtle message from Bill Belichick about individuals pulling their weight to avoid dragging the team down.

The coach had long preached the values of leadership, character and unity, and maintained that an abundance of these qualities would overcome adversity. Teams learned from distress, as they buried losses and moved on. Belichick added dramatic flare to his words when he and his team literally buried the football from the Dolphins loss. The coach was determined to sweep away panic, doubt and discord to create room in the Patriots clubhouse for poise, determination and production.

ABOVE LEFT PUNTER LEE JOHNSON LOSES THE HANDLE ON A WOULD-BE PUNT

BELICHICK HAD LONG PREACHED THE VALUES OF LEADERSHIP, CHARACTER AND UNITY AND HOW AN ABUNDANCE OF THESE QUALITIES

WOULD OVERCOME ADVERSITY

ABOVE BILL BELICHICK SAW THE COMEBACK WIN OVER SAN DIEGO ON OCTOBER 14 AS A CORNER-TURNER
LEFT TO RIGHT THE ANCHOR, CHARGERS DOUG FLUTIE AS PREY, THE DEFENSE, DAVID PATTEN, TERRY GLENN

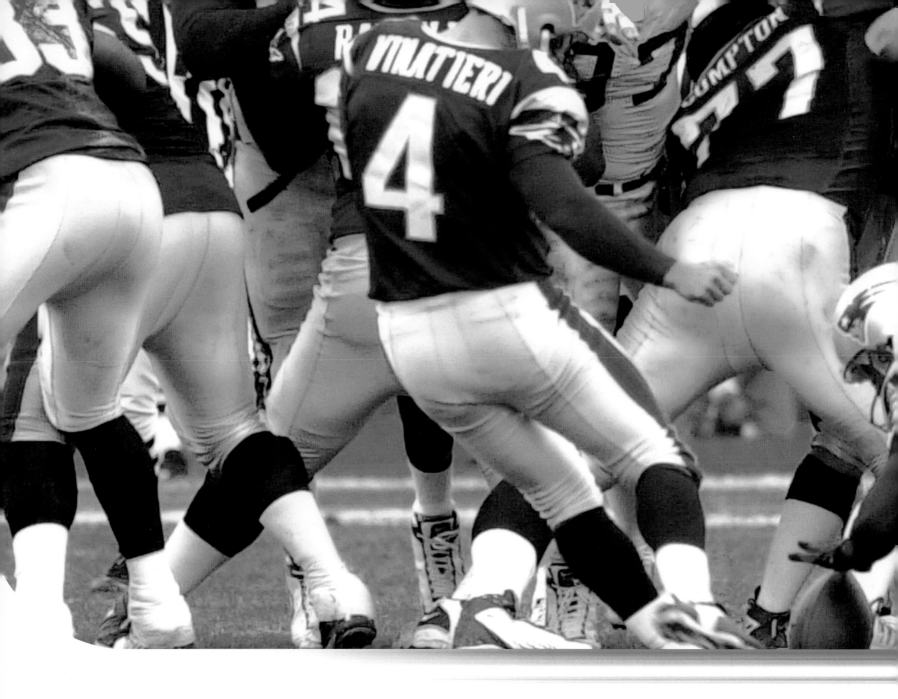

The challenge was great: Doug Flutie and the 3-1 San Diego Chargers were in town, with a three-game road trip to follow. The importance of November and December games is predicated on survival in September and October, and the Chargers game on October 14 truly represented desperation for the Patriots; one more loss could lead to January tee times.

New England, again in need of a boost, received it courtesy of an exciting, innovative aerial attack aided by Terry Glenn's return from NFL suspension, and the clutch play of quarterback Tom Brady, who induced a pulse into a lifeless team and refused to let the season slip away.

In the wake of the Miami loss, a confident Brady, indifferent to any criticisms of a young upstart speaking out of place, addressed the team in a players-only meeting and challenged his teammates to demonstrate more intensity in practice. He punctuated his exhortations with a 33-of-54, 364-yard, two-touchdown performance, guiding his club to a comeback 29-26 overtime win over San Diego. Brady stood tall in the pocket and fired bullets all over the field.

The Patriots and Chargers went toe-to-toe with the lead changing four times.

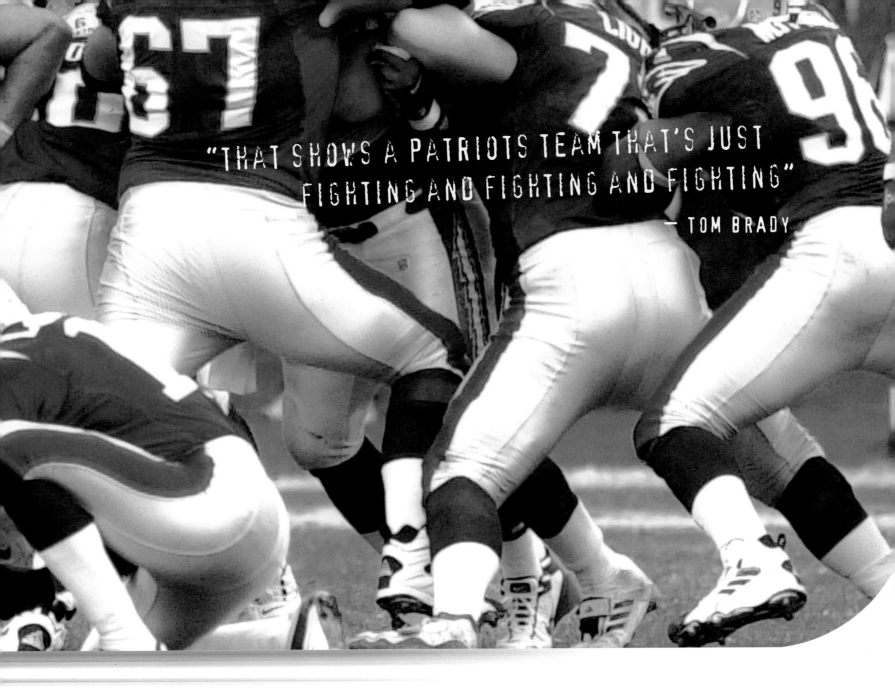

"THAT SHOWS A PATRIOTS TEAM THAT'S JUST
FIGHTING AND FIGHTING AND FIGHTING"
— TOM BRADY

San Diego led 19-16 when Patriots punter Lee Johnson, trying to sidestep a rusher, bobbled and then fumbled the ball, which was scooped up by the Chargers for a touchdown and a 26-16 advantage. This time, however, New England overcame the temptation to roll over and pulled out the victory in the fashion of a winning team going places.

A 15-play drive featuring a fourth-down conversion led to an Adam Vinatieri field goal to get back within seven. And, after the defense rose up and stuffed San Diego rookie running back LaDainian Tomlinson on third-and-one with 2:10 left, Brady engineered an eight-play, 60-yard scoring drive that tied the game courtesy of a 3-yard flip to uncovered tight end Jermaine Wiggins with less than a minute to go. Another defensive stop in overtime set the stage for Vinatieri's 44-yard field goal – his first game-winner of the year – to go along with Brady's first career comeback win.

"That shows a Patriots team that's just fighting and fighting and fighting," Brady said after the game. "I don't want to say the season is on the line because every week the season is on the line, but... we really fought our way out of a tough situation. That's the stuff you really build on as a team."

Brady's heroics weren't the only encouraging signs. Running back Antowain Smith inspired his teammates and the Foxboro Stadium crowd on a brutally tough 1-yard touchdown run, scoring after he was drilled squarely at the line of scrimmage by All-Pro linebacker Junior Seau. He absorbed the hit, bounced off and lunged into the end zone through a maze of mammoth bodies strewn on the turf in the aftermath.

Guard Joe Andruzzi, one week after being carried off the field with an apparent serious knee injury, was positioned between Damien Woody and Greg Robinson-Randall for the opening snap, displaying an infectious toughness once lacking in New England. Glenn's seven-reception, 110-yard effort proved his worth, and suddenly a versatile Patriots offense looked explosive with his brief appearance in the lineup. But it was Brady's words and actions that propelled the Patriots to victory.

"You come off a week like last week [in Miami]," Brady added, "and everybody tells you how bad you are and then you come off a week like this and people are telling you, 'Well you know they can really turn this thing around.' The important thing for us is that we are just concerned about what we think.

"We are concerned about going out to practice every day and focusing as hard as we can each week on the team that we are playing. We are 2-3 and we are going on the road now for three straight games and it is going to be a battle every week." With that, it was on to Indianapolis to take on the revenge-seeking Colts at the RCA Dome.

Lee Johnson's near-costly fumble led to his release. Ken Walter replaced him and would go on to enjoy a tremendous season. Then Glenn tweaked his hamstring late in the week, effectively ending his season. Finally, doctors cleared Drew Bledsoe to begin exercising and lifting weights, sparking the first signs of quarterback controversy in the media. Belichick rebuffed such talk.

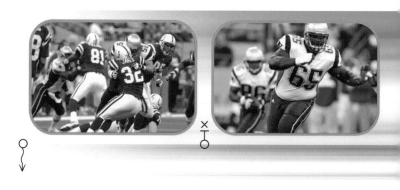

"He's not back on the field," he said. "He may be one day closer to being back, but that's not something that's going to happen this week or next week. When Drew's back to 100 percent, we'll deal with that then. But we're a long way from that now. The next step for Drew is to resume moderate to heavy physical activity to regain his skills at his position. Until that happens, it's way premature to talk about anything else."

Belichick's focus never wanders beyond the next opponent, and his players have learned to follow that lead. The Patriots throttled the Colts, 38-17, for the second time in three weeks, securing their first road win of the season. The Patriots scored on three one-play touchdown drives with David Patten completing a rare trifecta.

New England, benefiting from one of two blocked field goals, needed just one play – a 29-yard reverse to Patten – to make it 7-0. Midway through the second quarter, Brady planted in the pocket behind the line of scrimmage at his own 9-yard line and released a perfect strike just outside the left hash marks, hitting Patten in stride.

The diminutive wideout outraced the defense to the end zone for a 91-yard touchdown play – the longest in team history.

Patten completed the hat trick 1:45 later when he caught a pass from Brady behind the line of scrimmage, turned and lofted a perfect 60-yard spiral to Troy Brown for a 21-3 lead. Patten became the first player in 22 years to catch, throw and run for a touchdown in the same game, the previous being Hall of Famer Walter Payton, who had accomplished the feat for the Bears on October 21, 1979 – 22 years to the day.

The win, New England's third in four weeks, provided momentum. With the youthful Michigan product operating efficiently at the offensive controls, the Patriots were starting to believe.

"[Brady] doesn't get rattled," offensive coordinator Charlie Weis said. "He's made some big plays. When we've given him opportunities, he's made the most of them." Brady connected on 16-of-20 passes for 212 yards and three touchdowns against the Colts and had not thrown an interception in four games.

WITH THE YOUTHFUL MICHIGAN PRODUCT AT THE OFFENSIVE CONTROLS OPERATING EFFICIENTLY,

THE PATRIOTS WERE STARTING TO BELIEVE

Seeking three wins in a row for the first time since September of 1999, the Patriots traveled to Denver, where they squandered a pair of 10-point leads en route to a disappointing 31-20 loss. Brady was again sharp through three quarters and finished 25-of-38 for 203 yards, but his four fourth-quarter interceptions, one which was returned for a touchdown by Denard Walker, snuffed out any hope of late-game heroics. They were the first interceptions of his pro career and snapped a streak of 162 passes without an interception – the longest such NFL string to start a career.

The Patriots performed like a team that should have won rather than one simply fighting to stay close. It was a quality loss, if such a thing exists, and the team's last defeat a few weeks later would fit the same mold. It was obvious to all that the Patriots were evolving into a class outfit.

More devastating than the loss, was the injury to team captain and outspoken leader Bryan Cox, whose leg was broken on a cut-block by Denver offensive lineman Dan Neil.

"You have to get rid of the game by Monday night," Belichick said. "Coaches have to get rid of it. Players have to get rid of it. We have to bury the ball from Indianapolis just like we had to bury it from Miami. You have to erase the board and start getting ready with just as meticulous preparation and intensity as any other week, regardless of whether you win or lose. That's what being a real professional is. That's what a good professional team is. I hope that is what we're starting to become."

The Patriots confirmed their coach's hopes at Atlanta's Georgia Dome the next week. Pre-game hype centered on Brady's ability to overcome his four-interception fourth quarter in Denver – his first personal adversity as a professional. So the poised signal-caller simply shrugged off his doubters, as he had all season, to complete 21-of-31 passes for 250 yards with three touchdowns to three different receivers and no interceptions in the team's impressive 24-10 win. The victory staked New England to a 4-4 record at the halfway mark and just as importantly, 2-1 on the make-or-break three-game road trip.

The Patriots defense came alive on November 4 in Atlanta. It threw a ferocious, blitzing scheme at the Falcons and sacked quarterbacks Chris Chandler and Michael Vick nine times, knocking Chandler from the game with a shoulder injury. It was a 60-minute effort, without the problematic third-quarter woes that had plagued the team through the season's first half. The running game finally emerged behind Antowain Smith's 117 yards – his first 100-yard performance as a Patriot. And Lady Luck was finally in the Patriots camp when an errant Brady pass into triple coverage deflected off Atlanta's Ashley Ambrose into Troy Brown's hands for an easy 44-yard touchdown.

"IT'S NOT ABOUT WHERE WE ARE,

With the victory and a return to .500, the Patriots could think realistically about the post-season. With five of the last eight games at Foxboro Stadium, hope was restored for a Patriots Nation that had taken a turn to guarded optimism.

"It's not about where we are," Belichick stressed following the Falcons win. "It's about where we're going."

Did the coach know something in November? How clairvoyant was Brady when he quietly informed roommate and teammate David Nugent as early as mid-season that the Patriots were Super Bowl bound?

110

IT'S ABOUT WHERE WE'RE GOING"

— BILL BELICHICK

It was obvious to observers that New England was marching in the right direction, but no one besides Brady was making reservations for New Orleans.

The quarterback may have been second-guessing himself somewhat when the Patriots returned for a three-game home-stand starting with a hapless 1-6 Buffalo bunch.

New England nearly suffered a devastating letdown against the resilient Bills after a lengthy injury list forced scaled-back practices throughout the week. While the team never trailed in the game, New England needed a 42-yard touchdown run from Smith in the final minute to secure a shaky 21-11 victory.

Brady's performance that day showed that victory is not always supported by gaudy offensive statistics or performances. He was sacked a season-high seven times while completing 15-of-21 passes for an undistinguished 107 yards with a touchdown and an interception. Smith, conversely, finished strong, rumbling for 100 yards for the second straight week as the Patriots offensive line began to unite into a physical front that would be critical to the team's post-season success.

111

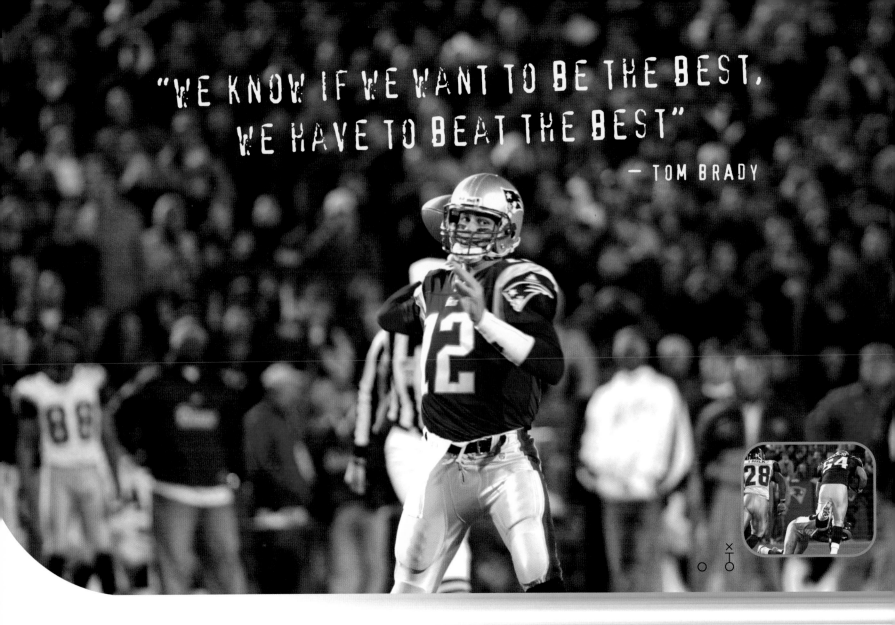

"WE KNOW IF WE WANT TO BE THE BEST,
WE HAVE TO BEAT THE BEST"

— TOM BRADY

The defense registered five sacks and two interceptions while knocking starting quarterback Rob Johnson from the game on a backside blitz by Terrell Buckley, who landed on the quarterback's shoulder. The team was above the fabled .500 mark for the first time since December 12, 1999 when it had stood at 7-6 before losing two straight. Belichick was on the winning side for the first time as Patriots head coach.

"I'm really happy for our football team," Belichick said. "They'd been written off by a lot of people and didn't get a lot of credit for how hard they've worked."

Team confidence was climbing even as the NFL's best, the high-octane, pedal-to-the-metal St. Louis Rams, invaded Foxboro Stadium on November 18. The 7-1 Rams promised to bring an accurate measuring stick to show exactly how far the Patriots had come.

"We know if we want to be the best, we have to beat the best," Brady said. "It'll be exciting for us. We are in front of our own fans and it is going to be a night game, and everyone is going to be watching. So we're going to put our best effort out there."

Brady's best effort was indeed needed with Bledsoe cleared by doctors to resume playing and anxious to reclaim his job.

Belichick wasn't about to make a quick change under center. "We expect Tom to play against St. Louis," Belichick said. "I can't answer any questions as to what will happen down the road. I'm not going to tell people not to talk about it, but that's not what it's about for me. It's about trying to win a game and trying to put the players out there on a weekly basis we feel we can win with. That's what it will always be about."

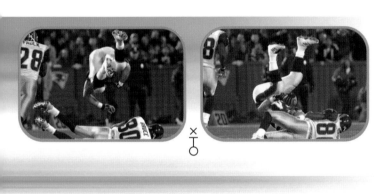

Both Bledsoe and Brady staved off any hint of controversy.

"There's no division, and we wouldn't let that happen," Brady said. "The one thing I would do to disrespect Drew would be to say, 'Here's your job back.' We're friends who come to work every day. We have a lot of support for each other. I'm confident that if I'm in the game we're going to win. If he's the quarterback, I know we're going to win." While Bledsoe picked up a few practice repetitions with the starters, Brady continued to take most of the snaps in preparation for the toughest test of the season.

Foxboro Stadium was abuzz for the team's only prime time Sunday night nationally televised game of the season, and the Patriots hoped a brisk November evening and a grass surface would slow Kurt Warner, Marshall Faulk and the St. Louis track team of speedy receivers Torry Holt, Isaac Bruce and Az-Zahir Hakim.

St. Louis drew first blood against New England's blitzing defense, but the Patriots responded with 10 points, seven coming on Buckley's 52-yard interception return for a touchdown. The game's turning point came just before half-time when Antowain Smith fumbled on the Rams 3-yard line with 2:12 remaining. St. Louis took advantage, driving 97 yards in eight plays and scoring the go-ahead touchdown on a 9-yard Warner-to-Faulk pass in the left front corner of the end zone. A potential 17-7 Patriots half-time lead had turned into a 14-10 deficit.

It was 24-10 when Brady guided a 65-yard touchdown drive to get within one score with 7:46 left in the game. But the powerful Rams, showing they could move the ball methodically on the ground as well as explosively through the air, held the ball for the remainder of the game.

The Patriots blitzed Warner 39 times, trying to pressure him into costly turnovers, but the rhythmic passer burned them throughout. With short drops and a quick release, Warner completed 30-of-42 for 401 yards with three touchdowns and two interceptions. While it wasn't as easy for Warner as the statistics might indicate, Belichick learned some things from watching the Rams quarterback spray the ball around against his pressure defense. That knowledge would lead to an entirely different game plan in their second meeting – a meeting St. Louis head coach Mike Martz came close to predicting in November.

After the game, Martz called the Patriots "a Super Bowl caliber team."

BROWN SHINES BRIGHTLY

0> *In deep traffic, Troy Brown* dodges would-be tacklers. One head fake right and juke left later and he is away, green expanse beckoning. **10>** *Brown's weekly heroics* have elevated him from overachiever to superstar. He is not the prototypical star NFL wide receiver. He's short at five-feet, ten-inches and lacks the deep blazing speed usually associated with the elite pass catchers. What he lacks physically, however, he more than accounts for with toughness, heart, intelligence and work ethic. **20>** *He eludes opponents,* breaks tackles and drags opponents for extra yardage and runs outstanding routes in search of open pockets, often losing two defenders in the process while boldly working the middle of the field. **30>** *When Shawn Jefferson left New England after the 1999 season,* critics said Brown couldn't be a number two receiver. All he did was catch a career- and team-high 83 passes for 944 yards and four touchdowns. In helping New England to its first Super Bowl title, Brown corralled a franchise-record 101 passes for 1,199 yards and five touchdowns. "He's our team MVP," said safety Lawyer Milloy. "He's what the Patriots are all about and what makes our team go." **40>** *Brown's astounding big-play return* skills enhance his pass-catching prowess, making him a potent double threat. He returned two regular season punts for touchdowns in 2001 – the first for 85 yards against Cleveland, and the second for 68 yards at Carolina. **50>** *He then thrust a dagger into the Pittsburgh Steelers Super Bowl hopes* with two jaw-dropping special teams plays at Heinz Field in the AFC Championship Game. He opened the scoring with a 55-yard punt return for a touchdown. And when he sprinted to and scooped up a loose ball bouncing free after a blocked field goal, having the presence of mind to lateral it to a streaking Antwan Harris for a touchdown, he ascended to cult status. **60>** *"He accounted for most of their points,"* Steelers safety Lee Flowers said. "The guy is a heck of an athlete and a special player. I think a lot of guys voted for him for the Pro Bowl." **70>** *When the Patriots needed a big play* during their final Super Bowl XXXVI drive, it was Brown who eluded the defense and caught Tom Brady's pass streaking over the middle before bolting out of bounds to stop the clock with the Patriots on the edge of field goal range. **80>** *"They were in a zone defense,* and I saw the middle linebacker dropping deep," Brown said. "On the other side of me was the dead spot in the zone and I knew I had to get over there to have a chance to get it. Tom did a good job stepping up and finding me and I was able to get out of bounds [to stop the clock]." **90>** *His reward was a championship* and a trip to Hawaii for his first Pro Bowl. Now the league realizes what New England has known for years. Troy Brown is a star.

TROY BROWN'S
SPECIAL
PERFORMANCE
IN THE AFC
CHAMPIONSHIP
KEPT PITTSBURGH
FANS SILENT

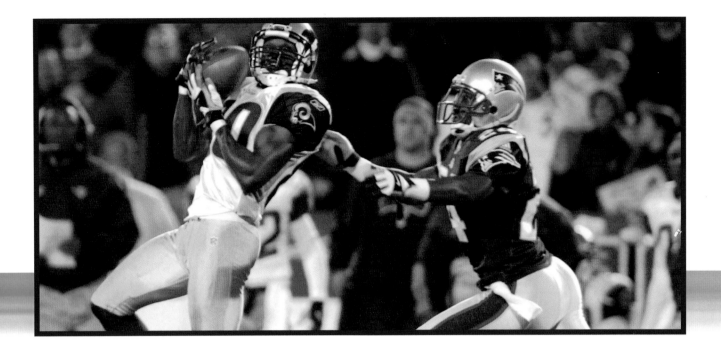

But were they as good as the Rams? *Boston Globe* columnist Ron Borges observed this: "[The Rams] are better. It doesn't get simpler than that in sports. The St. Louis Rams are better than the New England Patriots. Better on offense. Better on defense. Better at crunch time. Much better at crunch time, in fact. Better when games are won and when they are lost."

In Week 10, it was difficult to disagree with Borges' sentiments, but the Patriots players believed that without untimely mistakes, a win had been within reach.

"One of the things that came out of this is that we know we're a good team," cornerback Ty Law said of the Rams loss. "We had a chance to win the game, but we made too many mistakes. It's that simple."

"You think about those plays after the game and it was one we easily could have won," Brady added. "We're still in the game with 10 minutes left even though we made mistakes. We played against a real good football team and we're right there with them. But you hate to lose."

Belichick, however, found no consolation in the loss. "We expected to win, we expected to score points, we expected to play well defensively, we expected to play well in the kicking game and we came up short. That's disappointing and that is really the bottom line."

The feeling outside the Patriots locker room was that the game wasn't as close as the score – especially the way St. Louis controlled the clock to end the contest.

"We had an opportunity to shock the world," Smith said while absorbing heat for his critical fumble. "We had an opportunity to upset the Rams and show what we're made of."

Even in defeat the Patriots were evolving into a tough, determined team unseen in these parts since the days of John Hannah. After knocking quarterbacks Chris Chandler and Rob Johnson out of action the prior two weeks, New England's physical style sent six Rams to the injured list. That, as much as anything, sent a message to the league, but more importantly demonstrated how far New England had come since the lopsided pre-season loss to Tampa Bay.

In Week 11, that toughness would be put to the test against one of the league's more physical teams, the New Orleans Saints. The Patriots, however, were ready to flex their muscles.

ABOVE ISAAC BRUCE GETS BEHIND TY LAW

CHAPTER 7

BACK IN THE RACE

For all of his first eight seasons

in New England, a healthy Drew

Bledsoe started at quarterback.

He was a constant through roster

overhauls and coaching changes.

No matter what happened with

or to the Patriots, Bledsoe taking

the snaps represented stability.

He was tough, durable and productive. He directed the Patriots through their most successful period in history with four playoff appearances in five seasons, including the first-ever back-to-back-to-back berths in the post-season tournament from 1996 through 1998, with one AFC Championship to his credit.

Mo Lewis' devastating blow to Bledsoe's chest on September 23, 2001 changed everything. It altered the Patriots future. With second-year back-up Tom Brady taking over during Bledsoe's first lengthy absence from the line-up, the Patriots started winning – a possibility deemed highly unlikely as the nine-year veteran rode in an ambulance en route to Massachusetts General Hospital.

At 0-2 with Bledsoe out indefinitely, a wasted season had loomed. Two months later, however, the Patriots were 5-5 with a new leader directing the offense and a newfound optimism spreading through the clubhouse. Bledsoe could do nothing but look on as the second-year quarterback took over the team and ran it unlike any of Bledsoe's past substitutes would have.

Quarterback controversies can rip a locker room apart, destroy chemistry and cost a head coach his job. Factions develop and each week's result becomes a commentary on who should play. Conflict seemed unavoidable with Bledsoe's healthy return. Both choices facing Belichick were risky; re-insert Bledsoe into the lineup and possibly disrupt team chemistry, or leave a three-time Pro Bowler on the bench behind an unproven passer.

The loss to St. Louis was less than a day old when the Patriots turned their attention toward their next opponent, the New Orleans Saints. His rehabilitation over, Bledsoe prepared to reclaim his job and his team. That's when Belichick dropped a bomb on the hopeful veteran.

Belichick's announcement on the November 19 *Patriots Monday* radio program that Brady would remain the starting quarterback for the "foreseeable future" stunned and hurt Bledsoe, who felt a promised opportunity to compete for the job had been retracted.

Asked his feelings on the matter, Bledsoe tersely replied, "Next question." He later said, "I looked forward to the chance to compete for my job and I'll leave it at that." Bledsoe also said he "was told" he would get that opportunity, but it was obvious that Belichick had changed his mind.

In a November 21 press conference, Belichick elaborated on his decision to stay with Brady for the stretch run.

"This is not about Drew losing a job," Belichick said. "This is strictly about the team. It's about getting the team ready. I don't think you can get two quarterbacks ready. I feel that for us to get our starting quarterback ready we need to give that player the majority of the [practice] reps. When Drew was the quarterback, it was the same way."

Belichick refused to let the interests of one player, no matter how tremendous a person or performer that individual had been, supersede what he thought was in the team's best interest.

The head coach handled the toughest, most flammable situation of the season smoothly and the team's record in the weeks that followed confirmed that. With Brady at the helm, the Patriots never lost again, and it was another triumph in Belichick's brilliant coaching season – one many experts would rate as one of the best coaching jobs ever.

Although Bledsoe felt betrayed by his head coach, his decision to travel the high road also served the team well as it began an unlikely drive to a championship.

"My intention is to do the same thing I've done for nine years and ever since I was drafted by this team and that is to do whatever I can to help this team," Bledsoe said. "In this particular case, that means continuing as I have to help Tom on the field and help him during the week.

"One thing that falls into that category is to conduct myself in a manner that allows the players on this team to support both Tom and [me]. I feel like I've done that to this point and I don't intend to change," Bledsoe added.

His decision to do the right thing rather than disrupt a harmonious locker room helped the Patriots avert a potential disaster.

ON THE SIDELINE, THE INJURED BLEDSOE PROVED A FRIEND AND CONFIDANT FOR FIRST-YEAR STARTER BRADY

"THIS IS NOT ABOUT DREW LOSING A JOB
I DON'T THINK YOU CAN GET

– IT'S ABOUT GETTING THE TEAM READY.
WO QUARTERBACKS READY"

– BILL BELICHICK

"WE JUST WANTED TO GO OUT THERE

AND PLAY SMASH-MOUTH FOOTBALL"

— ANTOWAIN SMITH

ABOVE NEW ENGLAND SHOWED NEW ORLEANS WHO THE TOUGH TEAM REALLY WAS

"I take my hat off to the guy," defensive captain Lawyer Milloy said. "I know [if it were] me in that situation, being a veteran and losing my job to injury and trying to focus on the success of the team vs. my own individual opinions, [it] would be a hard apple to swallow. I probably wouldn't handle the situation as well, but I'm thankful to him that he didn't make it a distraction."

With all parties deflecting controversy, the unified Patriots sent the Saints limping back to New Orleans, victims of a 34-17 physical beating that served as a statement to the league.

Not only did Brady impress under the microscope with a 19-of-26, 258-yard, four-touchdown, no-interception performance, but a suddenly imposing offensive line blew the Saints tough front four off the ball, allowing Antowain Smith to pound away for 111 yards and a touchdown on 24 carries – his third 100-yard game of the month.

New England dominated from the outset, delivering the message that the old finesse Patriots were history.

That metamorphosis was one of several elements that made a championship possible, and while New England slowly developed into a physical group on both sides of the ball, the win over New Orleans was the team's coming-out party.

"All week we'd heard about how physical New Orleans is on defense and we felt we had a physical team also," Smith said. "We just wanted to go out there and play smash-mouth football."

When Brady rolled to his right and completed a 20-yard laser down the middle of the field to Charles Johnson for a touchdown and 20-0 lead with 10 seconds left in the first half, the Patriots march to the Super Bowl took its first steps.

While the offense pushed New Orleans around, the defense flew all over the field as well. Milloy picked off an Aaron Brooks pass and deflected another for an Anthony Pleasant interception. The NFL's third-leading rusher, Ricky Williams, was restricted to 15 carries for an inconsequential 56 yards.

LINING UP TOUGH

|0> **Facemask-to-facemask, eye-to-eye;** *so close that a simple breath is like a breakfast menu. It's Sunday at one o'clock. Time for NFL football, three hours of collisions and bone-shattering impacts. It's a test of manhood. Who is tougher? Who will win the unheralded battle in the trenches?* **1|0>** **Bill Belichick lectures about toughness;** *it is required of any job applicant. For far too long, the pass-first Patriots were a finesse team. That slowly changed in 2002, as Belichick's roster transformation infused meanness and toughness into a team needing the edge those ingredients provide.* **2|0>** **It started up front on the offensive line** *where veterans Mike Compton and Joe Andruzzi led young- sters Damien Woody, Matt Light and Greg Robinson-Randall, educating them on the strategies and tactics of hand-to- hand combat. The magnitude of offensive line cohesion was unmistakable over the season's second half. Bruising 230-pound running back Antowain Smith didn't have his first 100-yard rushing performance until Week Nine, but followed it with two more in the next three on his way to 1,157 yards for the season.* **3|0>** **His toughness was obvious** *in the red zone with most of his 12 rushing touchdowns coming on short-yardage, goal-line runs through defenders, not around them. The Patriots proved they could compete with the league's power teams against the Saints in Week 11, physically dominating New Orleans on both sides of the ball.* **4|0>** **"I think everyone knows New Orleans built its team around smash-mouth football,"** *rookie tackle Matt Light said.* "We tried to match their intensity because that's who they are and that's what we do. We proved we wouldn't take it. [Bill Belichick] wants a team that will hit anybody in the face. That's the best way to play football." **5|0>** **The Patriots defense, hardly the league's most heralded,** *won with tough players like Tedy Bruschi, Otis Smith, Bryan Cox, Lawyer Milloy, Bobby Hamilton, Anthony Pleasant and Richard Seymour. That unit slowed the high-flying St. Louis Rams offense in the Super Bowl by out-hit- ting it and disrupting it.* **6|0>** **"For our system, toughness is real important,"** *defensive coordinator Romeo Crennel said.* "We've always had tough teams. That's one of the reasons you bring in a Bryan Cox, Roman Phifer, Anthony Pleasant and Bobby Hamilton – those are all tough guys. Mix it in with a guy like Lawyer Milloy, who we brought in the first time we were here and you start to get your kind of guys with that physical, aggressive, tough mentality. Then you get them working together and you have a chance to have something special." **7|0>** **Hit hard, hit often and hit them into submission.** *That credo worked well for a Patriots team that evolved into a physical force. The Patriots were 3-4 when toughness started taking over in Atlanta. They were an incredible 11-1 after that.*

THE PATRIOTS
OFFENSIVE LINE
LED TO A REBIRTH
OF TOUGHNESS
IN NEW ENGLAND

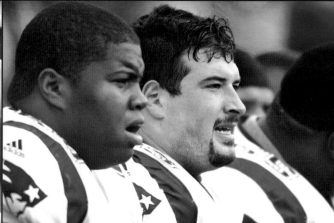

THE COMEBACK SHOWED YET ANOTHER
EXAMPLE OF THE PATRIOTS CHARACTER

"I think any talk of a quarterback controversy is now behind us," Milloy emphasized after Brady's NFL Miller Lite Player of the Week performance. "With a win like this, we know we can win with either one."

Milloy then told the *Boston Globe*'s Nick Cafardo: "A lot of people were talking about how we were going to respond after we lost to the Rams. Well, I like the way this team responded. I think we're going to be a dangerous team in the latter part of the season."

While Milloy's words eventually rang true in early February, the Patriots didn't seem very dangerous for the first 30 minutes of their rematch with the AFC East-leading New York Jets in Week 12, this time at Giants Stadium in the Meadowlands.

The Jets scored a touchdown on the game's opening drive and added a field goal on their second possession en route to a 13-0 half-time lead against a somnolent Patriots team.

New England's sputtering offense mustered only 67 first-half yards, and Brady was under constant pressure, forcing necessary half-time adjustments.

"We came in at half-time and the coaches challenged our manhood," fullback Marc Edwards recalled. "We were getting our butts whipped physically, and physical football was supposed to be the name of our game."

The Patriots came to life in the second half when a fortunate bounce went their way and they took advantage. Defensive lineman Brandon Mitchell deflected a Vinny Testaverde pass into linebacker Mike Vrabel's hands for a turnover and momentum changer. The offense adjusted to the Jets defensive pressure with shorter quarterback drops, and then turned to seldom-used Fred Coleman on a critical third-and-three play. Coleman took a short pass over the middle and raced upfield for a 46-yard gain to the Jets 4-yard line, setting up a 1-yard touchdown run by Antowain Smith.

125

DARK HORSES

|0> *Bill Belichick paused the tape.* Half of the 13-horse field scrambling for position four abreast around the race's final turn was frozen in mid-gallop. "Who will win?" Belichick asked his players. "Number two." "The blue one." Answers shot out from around the room as the Patriots watched a tape of the 2001 Breeders Cup Classic. "Who cares?" shot Belichick. "The race isn't over." **1|0>** *The Patriots were 7-5* and the tightly contested AFC East race was headed down the home stretch. It didn't matter that Miami and the Jets had nosed out in front of the Patriots. It wasn't over. **2|0>** *As Belichick re-started the tape,* the jockeys whipped their horses, challenging for every ounce of energy from the charging field. Three pulled in front down the final straightaway. Over the final 10 yards, a two-horse race emerged and culminated in a climactic, thrilling photo finish with horse of the year Tiznow winning at the wire. **3|0>** *The Patriots stretch run personified Tiznow's victory.* The team of the year stretched itself to the limit with a final surge characteristic of champions. They out-legged the Dolphins and Jets and then out-stretched the Rams at the wire. **4|0>** *A blown up photo from Tiznow's victory* hung over the stairs heading from the team offices to the locker room, serving as a reminder to the players to finish the race, which they of course did with a flourish. **5|0>** *A year earlier,* Belichick had watched almost helplessly as his team stumbled in the fourth quarter unable to close out opponents. He showed a valiant Secretariat galloping to victory in a textbook finish, but the equine analogy mattered little during a 5-11 campaign. **6|0>** *In 2001, with Belichick pulling all the right strings as the master puppeteer,* he asked his team to focus on finishing, so as not to waste the effort spent in gaining competitive position at the final turn. **7|0>** *He then watched with the pride of an owner* of a champion thoroughbred as his team headed for home and a world championship.

BILL BELICHICK, ALWAYS LOOKING FOR MOTIVATIONAL SYMBOLISM, FOUND SOME IN BREEDERS' CUP WINNER TIZNOW

The Jets responded with a field goal to make it 16-7, but the Patriots rallied. A 40-yard catch and run by Smith set up a 4-yard Edwards touchdown run, and an Adam Vinatieri field goal with 5:47 left gave New England its first lead, 17-16, and set up some late-game defensive heroics.

The exciting win, Belichick's first over New York since leaving that organization in January 2000, scrambled the AFC East race. With five weeks left in the season, Miami led the division at 8-3; the Jets were 7-4 and the Patriots 7-5.

With the playoff-contending Cleveland Browns coming to town, it was time for New England to surge.

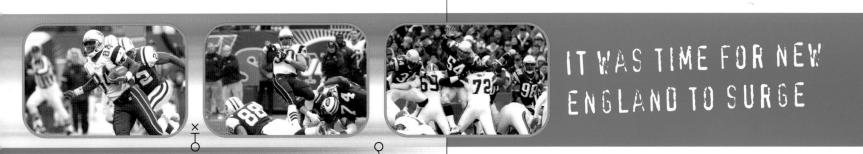

IT WAS TIME FOR NEW ENGLAND TO SURGE

With New York on the edge of field goal range and facing a third-and-five, the Patriots defense forced a quick incompletion and then Terrell Buckley intercepted Testaverde on fourth down to end the game.

The comeback was yet another example of the team's character and was an obvious season saver. "It was a turning point when we didn't shut it down, pack it up and get ready to go home on a train and be miserable [when we fell behind]," Vrabel said.

"We were down 13 points on the road and our season was on the line as far as competing in the AFC East," Belichick added. "We either had to get it done in the last 30 minutes or be looking down the barrel at the Jets."

Again, the Patriots started slowly and trailed the Browns, 10-3, after Brady threw an interception for a touchdown – a deficit that would have been larger if a Dennis Northcutt touchdown catch wasn't overturned by replay, forcing Cleveland to settle for a game-tying field goal.

The Patriots responded with two touchdowns, the second on Troy Brown's 85-yard punt return behind punishing blocks from Richard Seymour and Milloy. It was the first of three Brown punt returns for touchdowns over the next six games. New England struggled through the second half before a late Smith touchdown run iced it at 27-16.

With three games remaining, the Patriots found themselves in the thick of the division race, with two division rivals next up on the schedule.

127

THE PATRIOTS RESPONDED WITH TWO
85-YARD PUNT RETURN BEHIND PUNISHING

CHAPTER 8

A CHAMPIONSHIP CHARGE

BETWEEN CRAMMING FOR OHIO STATE'S

DEFENSE AND COMMUNICATIONS 101,

UNIVERSITY OF MICHIGAN QUARTERBACK

TOM BRADY LEARNED ONE OF THOSE

VALUABLE LIFE LESSONS THAT CAN'T

BE TAUGHT IN A LECTURE OR DRAWN UP

ON A CHALKBOARD DIAGRAM. IT WAS

A FOOTBALL LESSON THAT ACTUALLY

HAD NOTHING TO DO WITH FOOTBALL.

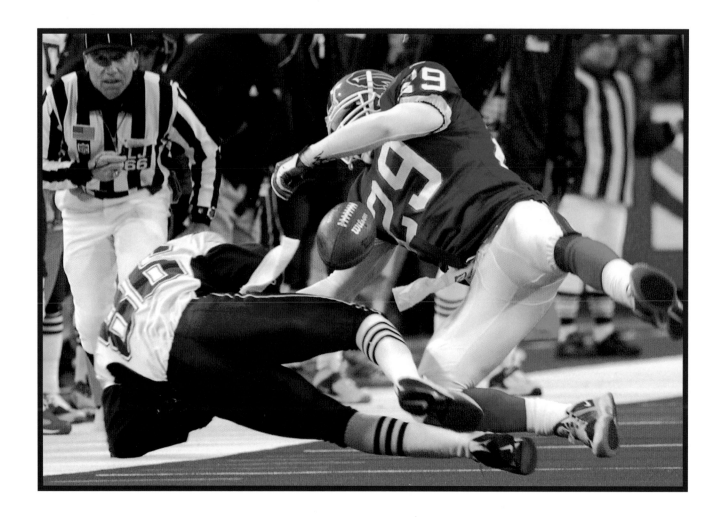

DON'T WORRY ABOUT THINGS BEYOND YOUR CONTROL

While sparring with phenom Drew Henson for playing time and warming the bench behind Brian Griese before that, the erudite Brady learned to focus only on those things within his control – priceless preparation for what would be a pressure-filled 2001 NFL season.

He toiled through rigorous off-season training as a fourth-string quarterback, readying himself to recognize opportunity whenever it knocked and answer it quickly. When it unexpectedly kicked his door in, Brady remained focused and worked tirelessly to improve his play, disregarding those critics who dissected the team's performance play-by-play.

Bill Belichick frequently delivers a similar message to his team, stressing short-term focus – a recycled version of the old "one-game-at-a-time" cliché. Belichick's bury-the-ball-and-move-on philosophy is based on the same principles that drive Brady.

Don't worry about things beyond your control.

For the New England Patriots, adhering to that axiom proved invaluable over the season's final weeks.

A so-called trap game awaited the 8-5 Pats in Week 14 as they shuffled off to Buffalo to battle the last-place, 2-11, Bills. The first meeting with Buffalo had been a street fight, and the second would be as well.

ABOVE   WITH DAVID PATTEN OUT OF BOUNDS AND HIS LEG ABOUT TO TOUCH THE PIGSKIN – DEAD BALL

Brady, claiming the unusually high crown on the Ralph Wilson Stadium turf affected his throwing mechanics, struggled throughout the chilly December afternoon in Orchard Park. He completed 19-of-35 passes for 237 yards with an interception, as New England's offense produced little against Buffalo's pressure defense. Brady's excuse drew criticism in New England.

With the defense stuffing Buffalo quarterback Alex Van Pelt, Brady finally found enough rhythm for a fourth-quarter, game-tying drive, and Vinatieri, who entered the game 5-for-12 lifetime in Buffalo, successfully booted a third field goal to send the game to overtime.

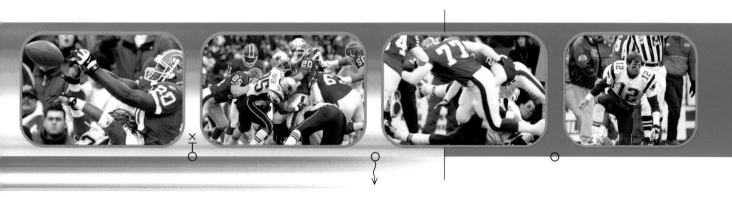

On the other side of the ball, the Patriots defense stifled an anemic Buffalo attack, and the result was a festival of field goals. Adam Vinatieri's two first-half kicks sent New England to the locker room with a 6-0 edge. The Bills rallied in the second half, dropping three straight kicks through the uprights, and held a 9-6 advantage with 5:57 left in the game.

The Patriots stingy red zone defense – solid all season – excelled throughout December when New England went 14 quarters during one stretch without allowing a touchdown.

"It might look like we're giving up a lot of yards," safety Lawyer Milloy said of the defense, "and we might not be the number one defense because of that, but we are resilient when we're in the red zone and we keep points off the board. We don't panic when they get down there."

That is when Lady Luck's magic graced the Patriots, courtesy of the obscure Rule 3, Section 20, Article 2, Paragraph C.

It happened this way. After stopping Buffalo to open overtime, New England appeared to turn the ball back over to the Bills after its initial possession. Facing first-and-10 at his own 46, Brady found wideout David Patten near the right sideline at the Buffalo 42, where Bills safety Keion Carpenter blasted him, forcing a fumble that Carpenter then recovered as Patten lay in a daze on the field.

The fumble call was challenged and replay showed that the ball was in contact with Patten's legs while the inert receiver's head and shoulders lay out of bounds, thereby making it a dead ball with the Patriots maintaining possession. Rule 3, Section 20, Article 2, Paragraph C.

133

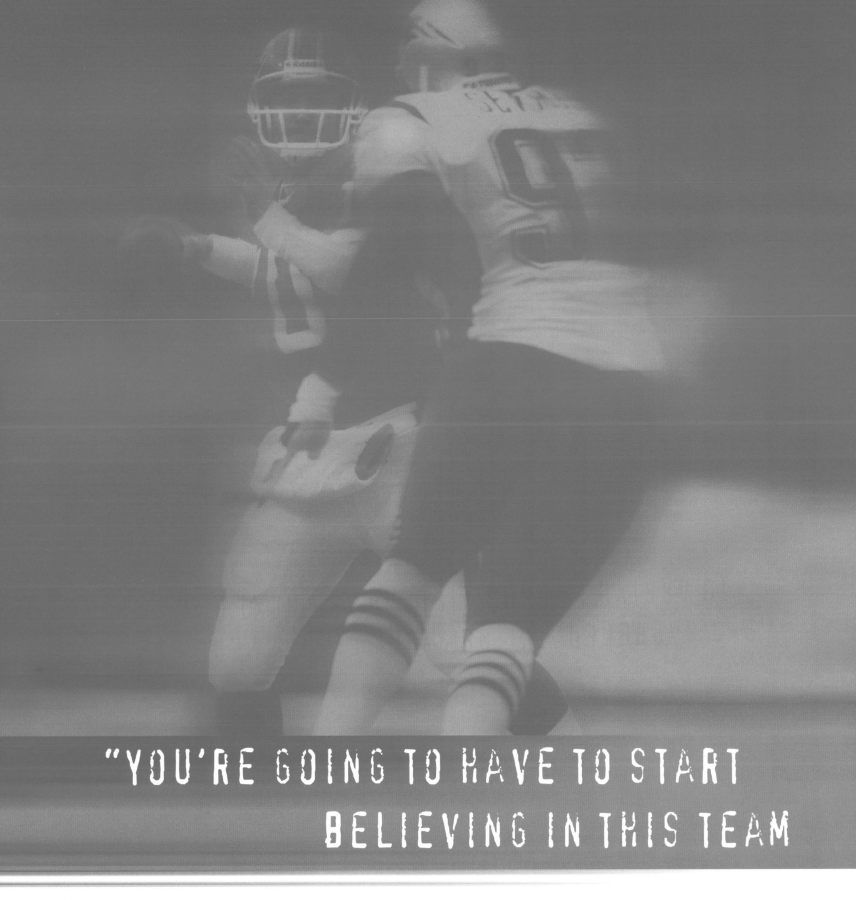

"YOU'RE GOING TO HAVE TO START
BELIEVING IN THIS TEAM

SOONER OR LATER"

— MIKE VRABEL

ABOVE RICHARD SEYMOUR CLOSES IN ON BUFFALO'S ALEX VAN PELT

Had Patten been conscious, he likely would have attempted an unsuccessful recovery, but more importantly, would have returned to the field of play in doing so. By virtue of being out cold, he never attempted to retrieve the ball and its contact with his body provided a new opportunity.

One play later, the Patriots took advantage of their second chance when Antowain Smith took a handoff to his left, reversed field to the right against the grain, and broke free for a 38-yard gain to the Buffalo 3-yard line, setting up Vinatieri's fourth and final field goal of the day and a bizarre 12-9 win.

"You're going to have to start believing in this team sooner or later," linebacker Mike Vrabel told the *Boston Herald*'s Michael Felger during the post-game glow.

The Buffalo win set up a first-place showdown against the 9-4 division-leading Dolphins in the final regular-season game ever played at Foxboro Stadium. "It's big," Milloy said of the Dolphins game. "Everyone can talk about the playoffs, but the number one goal you set the first day of training camp is winning the AFC East. It's what December football is all about."

DO YOU BELIEVE?

By Fred Kirsch, *Patriots Football Weekly* Publisher

0> *It doesn't take much for the fan* in this scribe to begin breaking down scenarios for the Patriots to win the Super Bowl. It pretty much happens at the beginning of each season. A good rush in Week One and I'm quietly researching which restaurants to visit in that year's Super Bowl host city. As the 2001 campaign got under way, all it took was a 44-13 pounding of the Colts in Week Three for me to start trotting out the "what-ifs?" The comeback win over the Chargers showed the team had heart. The physical beating they put on the Saints showed their toughness; the Jets win in the Meadowlands showed resilience. **1|0>** *The win over the Bills in Buffalo,* however, was what had me starting to believe that this thing was bigger than my annual jolt of optimism. That, of course, was the game where David Patten had his bell rung and saved the day by staying unconscious long enough for the referee to see that, after fumbling, his leg was touching the ball while his head and shoulders lay out of bounds. The Bills had recovered the loose ball but the dead ball rule allowed the Patriots to keep possession. One play later, former Bill Antowain Smith broke off a big run to put New England in scoring position for the win. **2|0>** *Strange and wonderful things began to happen* and it all culminated for me on the Northwest charter home from Carolina where the Patriots win had clinched the AFC East. Still, the question of a playoff bye was up in the air. The Patriots needed a Jets upset over the Raiders in Oakland for that to happen. So much had fallen into place for the team from New England so far that I was certain that this, too, was destined. It was part of the overall Super Bowl plan imprinted in my brain and I would accept no deviation. **3|0>** *The Jets/Raiders game was in progress* and scores were being updated sporadically by people squinting at vague images on mini-TV screens fuzzied by 30,000 feet. The best we could gather was that the game was close until someone across the aisle proclaimed, "It's over, the Raiders just won." "Damn," was the collective sentiment. The Patriots would have to play next week. Not the worst fate in the world but it wasn't the way I had it written. Something just wasn't right and I said so. "No, this can't be. This is not the way it's supposed to happen. The Patriots are supposed to get the bye. The Jets were supposed to win." **4|0>** *As usual, my ramblings were considered those of a madman* by my fellow travelers. A full 10 minutes passed with me muttering and shaking my head until a voice – the same one that announced the Raiders win – cried out, "The Jets just went ahead! John Hall hit a 53-yard field goal!" "Wait," I said. "You said the Raiders won." "I thought they did. The picture on the screen looked like they did." With that the plane jumped to life. Charlie Weis stood in the aisle with a TV; "Wait, wait. That's it, Jets won!" **5|0>** *Call it coincidence, luck, whatever.* But explain the following as reported by Shane Donaldson in Patriots Football Weekly. Coach Dick Rehbein, who tragically passed away during the 2001 training camp, had a little code he would leave for his wife and daughters at the end of messages left in various places – "143." It stood for "I love you," with each number representing the number of letters in each word. **6|0>** *Fast-forward to the Snow Bowl against Oakland* and the stadium holds its breath awaiting the referee's verdict upon review of Tom Brady's non-fumble. The play is overturned in the Patriots favor, but for some reason, the scoreboard clock is stuck on 1:43. The referee has to ask several times for the clock to be moved to the correct time remaining of 1:47. **7|0>** *There's more.* In the cavernous Louisiana Superdome, Pam Rehbein and her daughters find themselves sitting in none other than Section 143 for Super Bowl XXXVI. As half-time approaches, Tom Brady and David Patten – two of the players Rehbein was most instrumental in bringing to New England – hook up to make the score 14-3. Oh, and Brady's final record as a starting quarterback for the Patriots in 2001? 14-3. **8|0>** *Maybe it all meant something.* Maybe not. Either way, it works for me.

For the Patriots, it was the first time since 1998 that December football included legitimate championship aspirations. And with the Dolphins in town for a frigid Saturday matinee, New England sought to avenge the season's most embarrassing loss – the 30-10 debacle in Miami on October 7.

The Pats accomplished their goal behind Smith's bruising running and a physical brand of football that rocked the Dolphins and left them reeling from a 20-3 half-time deficit, too great to overcome in an eventual 20-13 loss. Smith hammered out 156 yards on 26 attempts while New England's defense forced and recovered three Miami fumbles on a day when heavy hitting and cold temperatures made ball handling difficult for the team from tropical South Florida.

Both offenses started sluggishly, and the Patriots provided the first spark late in the opening quarter courtesy of some trickery by offensive coordinator Charlie Weis.

It was third-and-one from Miami's 43 when Brady pitched out to Kevin Faulk, running right. Faulk stopped in his tracks and lofted a pass diagonally across the field beyond an over-pursuing defense to a wide-open Brady, who stepped out of bounds 23 yards downfield to set up the game's first touchdown. Brady later laughed about turning a sure touchdown into "only" a 23-yard gain thanks to his "blazing" speed.

ABOVE RIGHT "FIRST DOWN," SAYS WILLIE McGINEST VS. MIAMI
FROM LEFT TO RIGHT KEVIN FAULK, TOM BRADY, ANTOWAIN SMITH, TEBUCKY JONES

"THIS WAS THE MOST IMPORTANT GAME OF MY LIFE"
— ROMAN PHIFER

ABOVE   JAY FIEDLER AND TEAM FOUND A DIFFERENT PATRIOTS TEAM WAITING FOR THEM IN DECEMBER
THAN THE ONE THEY MET IN OCTOBER   **LEFT TO RIGHT**   BRANDON MITCHELL, TROY BROWN, DAVID NUGENT

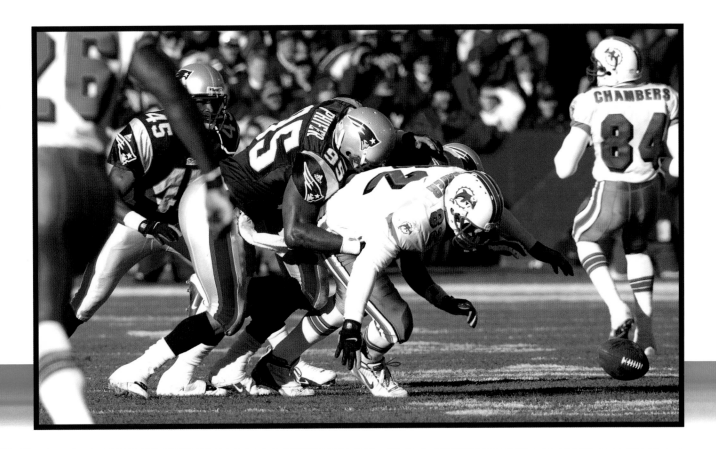

Miami actually had a chance to claw back into the game midway through the fourth quarter when, trailing 20-6, quarterback Jay Fiedler fired down the middle to running back Lamar Smith at the Patriots 3-yard line, but Tebucky Jones smacked Smith from behind, forcing a fumble that Roman Phifer recovered, thwarting the Dolphins charge.

Miami added a late touchdown, but it wasn't enough as New England celebrated a critical win over a longstanding rival. The Patriots headed to their bye in the AFC East driver's seat with only a Week 17 contest versus lowly Carolina remaining.

Multiple post-season scenarios were alive heading into the final week. It didn't take long for New England to advance; a New York Giants win over Seattle the day after New England's defeat of Miami, clinched the Patriots first playoff berth since 1998.

"This was," linebacker Roman Phifer told the Boston Globe's Nick Cafardo, "the most important game of my life."

"It's the first time in 11 years that I'll be going to the playoffs. I can't tell you what that means to me. I can't tell you how I feel right now because it's a feeling I don't think I've experienced."

"What a coaching job Bill has done," he added. "You appreciate it from the outside, but in here it's amazing to watch week after week."

The Patriots sat back and watched their rivals do battle in Week 16 as they rested and tended to their wounds. Smith, who suffered a leg contusion in his impressive performance against the Dolphins, was a particular concern as he was added to the injury list during game week in preparation for Carolina and sat out practice the week after the game.

Knowing they were in the playoffs, the Patriots could relax during their first off week since the September 11 tragedy and watch their counterparts jockey for playoff position.

ABOVE ROMAN PHIFER HAD A KEY FUMBLE RECOVERY IN THE DECEMBER 22 WIN OVER THE DOLPHINS

0> *The unexpected and unknown sometimes are special ingredients* in a championship formula, and that proved true for the champion New England Patriots. **10>** *Contributions came from every locker stall* in every situation. Wide receiver Fred Coleman contributed two huge plays down the stretch, an engine-starting catch and run to set up a touchdown in the Patriots comeback win in New York in early December, and a fumble-causing hit in kickoff coverage in the season finale win over the Dolphins. **20>** *How about punter Ken Walter* averaging 38.1 net yards per punt with 24 kicks downed inside the opponent's 20-yard line and only two touchbacks? The unexpected? Neither player was on the roster when the season began. **30>** *Rookies naturally represent the unknown,* and a pair of 2001 draftees, Richard Seymour and Matt Light, became impact starters. Seymour was a force on the defensive line's interior with 44 tackles and three sacks in 10 regular season starts, while Light protected Tom Brady's blind side throughout. **40>** *J.R. Redmond had hoped to secure the starting running back* job when training camp began, and was mildly disappointed at his opportunity. When his name was called, however, his versatility served the team well. As the regular third-down back, he repelled blitzers and made huge plays in crunch time against both the Raiders and Rams in the playoffs. His ability to squirt out of bounds in the final drive of the Super Bowl enabled the Patriots to continue the game-winning march with just enough time to spare. **50>** *The list goes on – a touchdown catch by Patrick Pass* against Miami. Jermaine Wiggins' 10 receptions in the snow against the Raiders. Antowain Smith's career revival and Brady's emergence. Terrell Buckley's big plays against the Rams and Jets. Greg Robinson-Randall's rock-solid presence and steady play at right tackle. Brandon Mitchell's blocked field goals, and a pair of fumble recoveries by Larry Izzo against Oakland. **60>** *Who will ever forget Antwan Harris' fumble-forcing hit in the Super Bowl,* Tedy Bruschi's evolution into a standout middle linebacker, and David Patten's priceless contributions, conscious and unconscious? **70>** *The Patriots were more than a team* that marched out of locker rooms as one. They were a team that relied on all 53 players, each ready to have his number called at any time. They didn't boast the most talented roster, but they evolved into a unit stronger than any assemblage of stars.

EVERYONE CONTRIBUTED. GUYS LIKE FRED COLEMAN, PATRICK PASS, JE'ROD CHERRY AND J.R. REDMOND ALL MADE THE MOST OF THEIR TIME

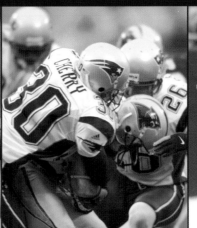

Things continued to fall into place while the Patriots sat idle as 2-12 Buffalo upset the Jets and Denver toppled Oakland, setting up an interesting final week in the AFC.

With a win over Carolina and a Jets win in Oakland on the season's final weekend, the Patriots would not only be the AFC East Champions, but also the number-two seed with its accompanying first-round bye.

Dame Fortune continued to favor New England in this magical season, as that exact scenario played out, paving an easier playoff road for a team that seemed destined to win in a year when wearing Patriots red-white-and-blue boosted spirits and elevated pride to previously unknown heights.

New England took care of its obligation with a sloppy, but convincing 38-6 season-ending win over the woeful Panthers.

The Patriots jumped out 10-0 on Ty Law's 46-yard interception return for a touchdown and Vinatieri's chip-shot field goal, and it grew ugly for Carolina in the second half. The magical Troy Brown returned a punt 65 yards for a touchdown, Smith scored on a 32-yard scamper off left tackle behind a punishing Marc Edwards block, and cornerback Otis Smith grabbed his second of quarterback Chris Weinke's three interceptions and scurried 76 yards for a touchdown.

Antowain Smith played through pain and ran for 81 yards on 21 carries while Brady wasn't particularly sharp in completing 17-of-29 throws for 198 yards with a touchdown and two interceptions. Six turnovers ultimately sealed Carolina's fate and secured a 15th consecutive loss in a single season, an NFL record for futility.

141

ABOVE JERMAINE WIGGINS FINDS OPEN SPACE IN THE PANTHERS END ZONE
BELOW TY LAW, OTIS SMITH, displaced NEW ENGLANDERS REJOICE

With the win, the Patriots celebrated their first division title since 1997 and boarded a plane for Providence, still unaware of their playoff destination.

At about 30,000 feet, New England's raucous players and staff celebrated the announcement that New York Jets kicker John Hall's 53-yard field goal had sunk the Raiders and given the Patriots the first-round bye and a home playoff game against either Oakland, Miami or Baltimore.

"To keep players used to contact and timing when you haven't been playing is a concern."

With another week off, Belichick took some time to reflect on the season and its turning points. "It was the fourth-quarter comeback against San Diego as much as anything," he said. "When you're 1-3 with a quarter of the season gone, you can't wait too long to make a move. Then you're down [10] points and you come back and win in overtime. That was a critical game."

"THERE WAS AN ELECTRICITY THAT IT CAUSED AND THE TEAM RAN WITH IT"
— BILL BELICHICK

With the silver lining comes some tarnish, or at least a lingering question or two. The good news was that the Patriots had a bye and a home game in the AFC semi-final. The bad news was, combined with the bye in Week 16 of the regular schedule, this would only be their second game in 29 days. Could New England use the additional time off or would the light schedule knock them off their game?

"[I was] more concerned with the time off we had between the Miami and Carolina games," Belichick replied.

But if there was one play, it came in the team's first win over Indianapolis in Week Three when Bryan Cox leveled Jerome Pathon like a wrecking ball. "I think that set a tone. There was an electricity that it caused and the team ran with it," Belichick said.

Up next: the Oakland Raiders, who upended the Jets in a Wild Card-round game to earn a trip to New England. The playoff excitement was about to begin.

ABOVE TROY BROWN SHOWS THE PANTHERS WHY YOU DON'T PUNT THE BALL IN HIS DIRECTION

ABOVE WILLIE McGINEST IS IN HOT PURSUIT OF A LOOSE CAROLINA BALL
BELOW PATRIOTS CELEBRATE THE AFC EAST TITLE WITH A DOUSING OF THEIR COACH

CHAPTER 9

A FURIOUS LAST FLURRY

It was fitting that it was the last

and greatest game in rickety

Foxboro Stadium's 31-year history.

And the old tenement went out

in Fifth Avenue style, puffing its

chest with pride, loyal to the

bitterly cold end.

Winter Wonderland, January 19, 2002.

Those who braved the frigid, snowy night fighting off frostbite and hypothermia while perched on those old aluminum benches found their early morning dreams filled with grand memories of an extraordinary night. Other unforgettable Foxboro Stadium moments survive like some indelible message scribbled on a bathroom wall. This one will forever be encased in museum-quality glass, written with a Mont Blanc pen on stately parchment.

It was the type of football New England children grow up playing, racing to the nearest sandlot or schoolyard as the first flake descends toward earth, fluttering downward in slow motion as a signal to round up the neighborhood to choose up sides. On this night, the commoner fondly recalled those games as his hero slipped and slid through packed powder.

Twenty-five years earlier in 1976, the Patriots had seemed poised to slam the door on the Raiders incredible 13-1 season. New England led 21-17 in the fourth quarter's waning moments when referee Ben Dreith flagged Ray "Sugar Bear" Hamilton for roughing quarterback Ken Stabler on a third-and-18 desperation pass.

It was a questionable foul known to New England fans as the "phantom roughing the passer" call and it provided Oakland with another chance at the end zone. The Raiders slipped by the bitter Patriots when Stabler scrambled for a touchdown with seconds remaining. Oakland went on to defeat Pittsburgh and Minnesota to win the Super Bowl.

Patriots fans never forgot. A playoff win over the Raiders in 1985 didn't atone for the blown call. But what happened on the frozen snow-covered Foxboro Stadium turf in the 2001 playoffs laid to rest a quarter century of ill will.

EVERYTHING PACKED INTO ONE GAME:

It was a game for the ages and for all ages – one of those nights Mom and Dad extend bedtime so junior can fend off the sandman to take in the big game with the family.

Everything packed into one game – playoff intensity, drama, rivalry, excitement, anxiety, controversy, heroics, blizzard conditions and overtime – it had it all.

It was pure pigskin theater. The marquee read AFC Divisional Playoffs – Raiders at Patriots, 8 p.m.

Sounds simple. But this was *Les Misérables* on football's concrete stage. This was American entertainment at its best. It was justification for outlandish salaries and rising consumer costs. The pre-game hype only added to the game's mystique.

PLAYOFF INTENSITY, DRAMA, RIVALRY, EXCITEMENT, ANXIETY, CONTROVERSY, HEROICS, BLIZZARD CONDITIONS, OVERTIME

- IT HAD IT ALL -

ABOVE CHARLIE WEIS AND TOM BRADY LEFT TO RIGHT TROY BROWN FUMBLES, LARRY IZZO RECOVERS, J.R. REDMOND, LAWYER MILLOY, HEAD GROUNDSKEEPER DENNIS BROLIN CLEARS THE LINES

0> *In training camp,* the Patriots list of veteran wide receivers included Troy Brown, Terry Glenn, Bert Emanuel, Charles Johnson, Torrance Small and David Patten. All but Patten, the diminutive receiver recommended by Dick Rehbein, were established veterans with significant NFL starting experience. **1 0>** *Of course, that only makes Patten's emergence from nowhere* a perfect fit in the Patriots scheme of things in 2001. The fifth-year receiver entered the season with 106 career catches in four years, including 55 in the last two combined. Not only did he scale the depth chart and evolve into a solid starter for New England, but he also became an essential component of a championship team. **2 0>** *Patten caught 51 passes* during the regular season and doubled his career touchdown total to eight from four. In the post-season with defenses smothering Brown, Patten elevated his game and built a reputation as a clutch, big-game performer. **3 0>** *In the Snow Bowl playoff game against Oakland,* Patten snared eight Tom Brady passes for a team-high 107 yards, including a huge fourth-down conversion on the game-winning overtime march. He also caught the only Patriots post-season touchdown passes – an 11-yarder from Drew Bledsoe in the AFC Championship Game, and an 8-yarder from Brady in the Super Bowl. Both scores came just before half-time and sent the opponent limping to the locker room trying to recover. **4 0>** *"I wasn't surprised* that David emerged," wide-out Troy Brown said. "I watched him work hard on the field and in the weight room. I saw how smoothly he caught the ball and ran routes. Combine that with his speed and I knew he could be a good player with the right opportunity. He got it and he stepped up and performed at a high level, especially in the clutch during the playoffs." **5 0>** *If any Patriots receiver* rivaled Patten's unexpected playoff heroics, it was tight end Jermaine Wiggins, the local boy from East Boston. Wiggins was a red zone specialist during the season, grabbing only 14 total passes, but with four touchdowns among them. All he did was set a Patriots post-season reception record against Oakland with 10 catches for 68 yards, proving effective in the blowing snow as he did in similar conditions in Buffalo a season before – his New England sandlot football roots obviously paying dividends. This performance prompted Head Coach Bill Belichick to dub him "our Snow Plow." **6 0>** *The Snow Plow* totaled 14 receptions in three playoff games, equaling his regular season output and finishing second among Patriots receivers behind Brown's 18. His final grab was the ultimate scene-setter, a 6-yard pass to the St. Louis Rams 30-yard line that set up Adam Vinatieri's Super Bowl-winning kick. "Like Patten, Wiggins stepped up and made big catches for us at big times," Brown added. "That's what defines a big-time player. You always have to be ready to make a play even if you aren't the primary receiver, and he came through for us." **7 0>** *Brady, Brown and Antowain Smith* may have garnered many of the offensive headlines in 2001, but the post-season contributions of Wiggins and Patten were priceless components of a world championship team.

DAVID PATTEN AND JERMAINE WIGGINS WERE TWO OF THE FIRST-YEAR PATRIOTS TO FIND THEIR WAY THROUGH THE SNOW

"WE'RE GOING FOR A CHAMPIONSHIP AND THEY'RE IN OUR WAY"

— LAWYER MILLOY

The Patriots-Raiders rivalry is much more than Dreith's blown call. It is Jack Tatum's paralyzing blow to Darryl Stingley, Matt Millen's punch at Patrick Sullivan. It is East Coast vs. West Coast and the abominated Silver and Black. This match-up also featured defense vs. offense in Bill Belichick vs. Jon Gruden – two driven men known to camp out in their offices cuddled up to a video screen until sunlight becomes painful to the eyes – hermits who live to outwit and outfox an opponent.

Patriots safety Lawyer Milloy sent an early salvo across the bow of the good ship SS West Coast when he warned Raiders future Hall of Fame wideouts Tim Brown and Jerry Rice to prepare for a physical flogging.

"I watched that game last week, and the [Jets] treated those guys like Hall of Famers – they hardly hit them," Milloy told the *Boston Globe*.

"When I'm out there, I'm not going to see numbers or credentials. If they come into my territory, they are going to get hit. We're going for a championship and they're in our way."

The snow had been falling for about four hours and showed no signs of relenting as the teams kicked off Round Two of the 2001 NFL post-season. The field was a slippery, white carpet packed with two or three inches of fresh powder as head groundskeeper Dennis Brolin and his Foxboro Stadium crew worked diligently with leaf blowers to keep the yard-line markers clean, albeit in vain.

The blustery wind whistled down through the stadium creating a blinding northeastern whiteout. The game-time temperature was 25 degrees, the footballs were rock-hard and the playing surface was more suited to the beloved Bruins than to the Patriots.

153

As bodies slid through the drifts piled up between the barely-visible 5-yard lines, and feet flew out from under normally sure-footed athletes, the teams wrestled with the elements, each waiting for the other to falter. The Patriots blinked first early in the second quarter when Oakland quarterback Rich Gannon hit seldom-used wideout James Jett in the back right corner of the end zone for a 7-0 lead.

The Patriots found the scoring column on the second half's opening possession when Tom Brady completed 4-of-5 passes for 65 yards, setting up Adam Vinatieri's 23-yard field goal.

Oakland seized control with two Sebastian Janikowski field goals driven through the blizzard to make it 13-3 as the fourth quarter opened. The Nor'easter gripping New England appeared to be choking the life out of the Patriots as conditions worsened in the snowbound stadium.

At least four inches of snow lay on the ground when an eerie series of events began, leaving all present shaking their heads in disbelief and trusting that something special was indeed in store for these Patriots. It began when sure-handed Troy Brown fumbled not one, but two fourth-quarter Shane Lechler punts; only to have teammate Larry Izzo fall on both. Ironically, those two recoveries started the team's scoring drives in the final period.

Just as hope gave way to grief, Brady's white-hot arm began heating up the offense. He connected on nine consecutive passes, mostly to wideout David Patten and "snow plow" tight end Jermaine Wiggins, for 61 yards. He completed the drive with a 6-yard touchdown run and a celebratory spike that sent him tumbling through the snow. It was 13-10 with 7:52 left.

The game was still Oakland's to win.

Facing a third-and-one with 2:19 to go and New England out of timeouts, the Raiders handed to bullish short-yardage running back Zack Crockett, who was stuffed short by Bryan Cox, Tedy Bruschi and Ty Law, forcing a decisive punt.

That series set the stage for the NFL season's most controversial play. It was first-and-10 for New England at the Oakland 42 when Brady dropped back to pass. Raiders cornerback Charles Woodson flew into the backfield off the left end and rocked Brady across his body and head, forcing the ball to squirt loose into the snowy tundra, where Oakland linebacker Greg Biekert recovered.

The game and the Patriots magical worst-to-first season seemed over. But with the game in its final two minutes, the replay officials in the press box called for referee Walt Coleman to review the play.

There was no way it could be overturned. Brady went to the sideline, watched the replay on Foxboro Stadium's jumbo screen and excitedly asked Charlie Weis for the next play, certain the call would go New England's way.

Coleman returned from the sideline with the hopes of sixty thousand quiet souls hanging on his words.

"After reviewing the play, the quarterback's arm was going forward; it was an incomplete pass," Coleman announced.

"Obviously, what I saw on the field, I thought the ball came out before his arm was going forward. Then, when I got to the replay monitor and looked at it, it was obvious his arm was coming forward. He touched the ball. And they just hooked it out of his hand. His arm was coming forward, which makes it an incomplete pass," Coleman explained after the game.

The frozen fanatics filling Foxboro Stadium exploded into a joyous frenzy, high-fiving, hugging and rejoicing chaotically as the resuscitated Patriots offense trotted back into the warmth found only in their huddle. Brady to Patten for 13 yards gave the Patriots a first down at Oakland's 29. Two incompletions and a 1-yard pass later, Vinatieri was hurrying onto the field for the most important kick of his life.

With no timeouts to clear a spot on the snow-covered surface, Vinatieri lined up with ice in his veins and on the field and booted a low line drive 45 yards through driving snow just over the cross bar to tie the game, 13-13, with 27 seconds remaining.

"I line-drived it, but when I looked up, I knew it was going to be straight enough," Vinatieri described his tying field goal.

"It can't get any tougher than [that 45-yarder] in four inches of snow and with the conditions and pressure of the kick, but we didn't have any choice," Bill Belichick said. "It was our only shot so we had to take it. We have a lot of confidence in Adam and he came through."

KNOW ANY OTHER WAY TO DO IT"

— BILL BELICHICK

THE GOLDEN TOE

By Steve Sabol, President, NFL Films

|0> **The Patriots trailed the Raiders** 13-10 in the 2002 AFC Divisional Playoff. With 32 seconds left to play, holder Ken Walter brushed the snow from the spot where he would place the ball for a 45-yard field goal attempt. The odds against this kick succeeding were piling up like the falling snowflakes. Sixty thousand Patriots fans squinted through the blizzard toward the distant goal post and hoped. 1|0> **A dramatic vision of the present** was about to become a memory for all time. Responsibility descended upon kicker Adam Vinatieri with a weight far beyond anything he had ever felt. Could he overcome the elements, the pressure, and the circumstances? Pressure defines the essential nature of athletic heroism. This is what the game asks of a man – what will you do when it counts? 2|0> **"I line-drived it,"** said Vinatieri, "and then I had to wait a second to see if it was going to go over the bar." It did. And Adam Vinatieri had delivered as romantic a moment as the city of Boston has ever known; from Foxboro into folklore. 3|0> **I believe it was the greatest kick in NFL history.** It was more difficult than Matt Bahr's 42-yard game-winner that brought the Giants from behind to beat the 49ers, 15-13, in the 1990 NFC Championship. It was longer than Dolphin Garo Yepremian's 37-yard overtime kick to beat the Chiefs in the 1971 AFC Divisional Playoff, the longest game ever played. 4|0> **Its eventual historical significance** surpassed Pat Summerall's epic 49-yard blast in snowy Yankee Stadium that beat the Browns on the final Sunday of the 1958 season, forcing a playoff for the Eastern Conference crown the following week, which the Giants won. 5|0>

And of Vinatieri's memorable game winner at the end of Super Bowl XXXVI, Adam himself said, "the Super Bowl kick was special, but the one in the snow at Foxboro was harder." So difficult, in fact, that the name Adam Vinatieri will be linked forever with a kick so stunning and incredible as to make believers of dreamers everywhere.

ADAM VINATIERI
WINS YET ANOTHER
GAME FOR HIS
CHAMPIONSHIP-
BOUND TEAMMATES

The greatest kick in NFL history kept the Patriots alive and well and headed to overtime – the 16th time since 1958 an NFL post-season contest needed an extra session to determine a winner.

The Patriots won the overtime coin toss, and Oakland never touched the ball again. Brady guided an almost anticlimactic 61-yard drive to open the period, completing eight straight passes, including a critical fourth-and-four conversion to finish the night 32-of-52 for 312 yards.

J.R. Redmond's 20-yard catch and run through a multitude of tired Raider defenders started the drive rolling, and the fourth down conversion broke Oakland's back. Vinatieri, fittingly, finished off the Raiders season at 11:35 p.m. EST with a 23-yard chip shot that sent a triumphant Foxboro Stadium into exultation and long snapper Lonie Paxton into a non-choreographed snow angel display in the end zone.

"I'm just so happy for our football team and those guys," Belichick said. "They just keep fighting. They don't know any other way to do it."

The Patriots were on their way to the AFC Championship game as the doors were closed on a stadium that most definitely had saved its best for last.

ABOVE RIGHT NEW ENGLAND MINUTEMEN DO THEIR BEST VALLEY FORGE IMPRESSION IN THE FOXBORO SNOW
BELOW OAKLAND'S GREG BIEKERT RECOVERS THE TOM BRADY NON-FUMBLE AND THE PATRIOTS SEASON GOES ON HOLD

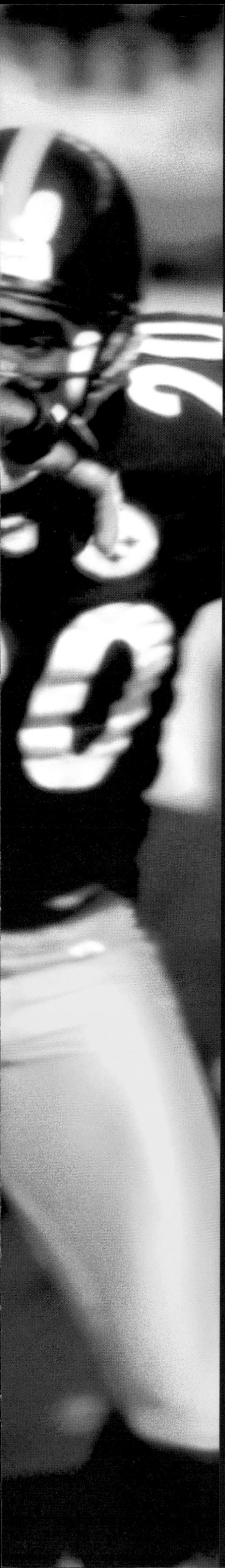

CHAPTER 10

FORGING RESPECT IN PITTSBURGH

TALK ABOUT NO RESPECT. THE NEW ENGLAND PATRIOTS, PRO FOOTBALL'S RODNEY DANGERFIELDS, WERE ON A ROLL, HAVING WON SEVEN STRAIGHT INCLUDING A GAME FOR THE AGES IN BLIZZARD CONDITIONS AT FOXBORO STADIUM.

Yet the entire football world seemed poised to anoint the 14-3 Central Division champion Pittsburgh Steelers, hosts to the AFC Championship Game at brand-new Heinz Field.

Prognosticators loved the black-and-gold lunch pail gang from The Steel City. They had the NFL's top-ranked defense and third-ranked offense. They had a vaunted rushing attack, a pair of 1,000-yard receivers and a Pro Bowl quarterback. They had the 12th man, were 10-point favorites and were most

certainly Super Bowl bound. Better still, they had a Super Bowl pedigree.

All you had to do was ask the Steelers or anyone else in Pittsburgh... or anyone in New Orleans, for that matter. The official Super Bowl game programs had been delivered to the city of Three Rivers with a note attached, "Do not open until Steelers win AFC Championship."

Not if. When.

162

New England's chances were apparently so negligible that rumors had it that the Fairmont Hotel in New Orleans, home to the AFC champs, already was adorned in black and gold, ready to greet its Pittsburgh guests for a week's stay. The coach's office within the hotel was labeled, "Head Coach Bill Cowher."

Their tickets were punched, their reservations made. Made publicly, in fact. The Steelers never shied away from premature Super Bowl speak, with quarterback Kordell Stewart even discussing a return home to New Orleans to play for the title.

Talk about no respect.

The Patriots organization discreetly made its necessary Super Bowl preparations, but the players were not privy to any details. They were to take care of their own business in Pittsburgh while behind-the-scenes staff members like Trent Adams, Jim Wilson, Rick O'Hare, Mike Nichols, Jen Ferron and Nick Carparelli, among others, tended to Super Bowl business outside the spotlight.

"OUR TEAM IS NOT A TEAM OF DESTINY.

Pittsburgh's sports world, meanwhile, focused its efforts on the Rams and a trip to New Orleans. No mention of the Patriots. The local newscasters wore Steelers game jerseys. Terrible towels fluttered by the thousands in the streets the night before the big contest. One zealous fan directed his screaming at a contingent of New England sports media on the field before kickoff. "You're not gonna come in our house and steal one! Not today, baby!" he bellowed.

But the Patriots decided to show up anyway, arriving at their team hotel outside Pittsburgh to a serenade of "Let's Go Steelers!" from a chorus of leather-lunged teenyboppers in black-and-gold.

And then there was the T-shirt – the one that hung in the Patriots locker room before and during the game. It was a Super Bowl XXXVI shirt – Rams vs. Steelers, of course.

No mention of the Patriots anywhere. No respect.

Meanwhile, New England's players shunned all mention of favorite media terms like destiny and luck. To a man, the players felt that the clichés diminished a team's success and potential.

"Our team is not a team of destiny," safety Lawyer Milloy proclaimed in his Friday AFC Championship press conference. "This is a team trying to take advantage of being a good team. I know the focus is on the other three teams that have a chance to compete for that trophy at the end of the year. Our focus has always been on us. Go ahead and overlook us. We watch ESPN. We watch the playoff commercials. They have all the other teams on there and I don't see one guy from our team. They have guys on talking about playoff experience and atmosphere, and it's guys who haven't even been in the playoffs before. It's crazy."

Each and every example of disrespect or neglect was an additional lump of coal added to a Patriots fire that was quietly reaching incandescence. And heat was the last thing needed on the spring-like but breezy January 27 in western Pennsylvania – the blue-collar site for two workmanlike teams to battle for AFC supremacy.

Perhaps they couldn't comprehend the kind of character forged in those New England hills in mid-winter. Perhaps all that talk of Walden Pond and the like was a touch too gentle for the rest of the country. The team emerging from the dark hills at dusk in New England had an attitude, from all first-team players down to the third and fourth men on the depth chart. This team had that look in its eye, and nobody noticed.

One player with a family, economy-sized box of attitude was the team's "new" back-up quarterback. It had been a trying year for Drew Bledsoe. He suffered a life-threatening chest injury in Week Two and then watched powerlessly as Brady directed and resurrected a franchise he had helped build and rebuild over nine seasons.

THIS IS A TEAM TRYING TO TAKE ADVANTAGE OF BEING A GOOD TEAM"
— LAWYER MILLOY

The Steelers had dined out for three decades on their blue-collar legacy, going back to four Super Bowls won by the likes of Bradshaw, Greene, Ham, Harris, Swann and Lambert. They owned the patent on black-and-blue and represented a formidable challenge to the team from the pastoral climes of genteel New England. That's how they thought of the Patriots in Steelerland. Harvard's team. Tea and crumpets on the quad. Regattas on the Charles. Finger sandwiches with no crusts. Busloads of blue-haired matrons packing buses on fall foliage tours.

His return to health didn't coincide with a return to the field as he angrily took a back seat to Tom Brady, while remaining the class act that arrived in New England in 1993. Displeased, he still supported Brady and the team, refusing to stir up the locker room and unsettle the team's chemistry with his own agenda. Rather than disrupt, he continued to prepare as Brady had in his own reserve role, knowing he was one play away from a meaningful return to action.

That play came late in the AFC Championship Game's first half when Steelers safety Lee Flowers rolled up on Brady's ankle as he completed a 28-yard strike to Troy Brown with 1:40 left in the second quarter, sending the second-year success story to the bench. Bledsoe, the owner of nearly every franchise passing record and arguably the most successful quarterback in team history, was back.

He had been out of sight, out of mind while the Patriots powered forward. The team never could win consistently without him during his career, and when it did so in 2001, his stature was somehow minimized, his legacy diminished.

Destiny or no, it was as if Bledsoe deserved one more shining moment, one more glorious day in the sun – an exclamation point on his Patriots career and a chance to go out with the class he displayed throughout. He trotted out before 64,704 hostile Steelers fans, looking to return to the Super Bowl, clapping his hands, re-introducing himself to the huddle and preparing to shake off the rust while Patriots Nation held its breath.

When he rifled his first pass into David Patten's chest for 15 yards to the Pittsburgh 25, a nervous mumble overtook Heinz Field and a collective cheer engulfed New England. Bledsoe was indeed back.

ABOVE DAVID PATTEN CATCHES DREW BLEDSOE'S FIRST TOUCHDOWN PASS SINCE SEPTEMBER 9, 2001

On his second play, Bledsoe scrambled to his right just as he had on the fateful September afternoon that changed everything. As he sprinted toward the sideline, cornerback Chad Scott got an angle and left his feet, drilling Bledsoe to the ground just as Mo Lewis had four months earlier. The similarities were eerie until Bledsoe jumped up clapping, as if the blow had energized him. He then channeled that energy, hit Patten for 10 yards, and once again in the corner of the end zone for an 11-yard touchdown and a 14-3 half-time lead.

who darted forward, zigged, then zagged, before speeding off on a 55-yard touchdown and a 7-0 tension-easing lead.

It was still 14-3 midway through the third quarter when the Patriots incredible special teams delivered a debilitating blow to the Steelers midsection. Pittsburgh was attempting to cut into New England's lead with a 34-yard field goal when Brandon Mitchell sliced through the protection to block Kris Brown's attempt. Troy Brown fielded the ball on a hop and sprinted forward.

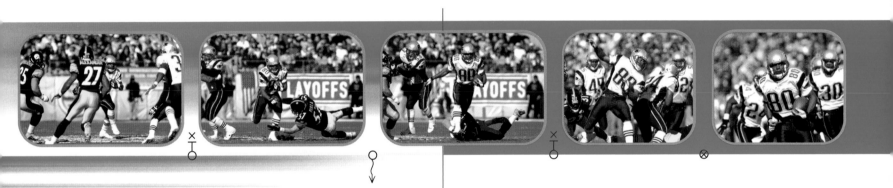

Bledsoe's record off the bench to date: three completed passes for 36 yards and a touchdown. It was the message to his team that the New England Super Bowl Express was still on the rails.

The first half was actually a microcosm of the season, with the opportunistic Patriots making the most of their chances. Opportunity arose late in the first quarter when Josh Miller's booming 64-yard punt that dribbled out of bounds at the Patriots 23 was called back because Troy Edwards was flagged for running out of bounds. Miller's re-kick failed to find the sideline and, instead, found the dangerous Brown,

With Pittsburgh's kicker desperately clinging to the Patriots diminutive giant, he alertly lateraled to Antwan Harris, who sprinted untouched to the end zone for a 21-3 lead.

From there, it was up to Kordell Stewart to bring the Steelers back, which he nearly did before self-destructing as the Patriots hoped he might.

He led two consecutive third-quarter touchdown drives to make it 21-17 with 16:29 left in the game. Adam Vinatieri's 44-yard field goal extended the Patriots lead to 24-17 with 11:12 remaining, after which the Patriots once-suffocating defense returned to form.

AGAINST ALL ODDS IN PITTSBURGH

By Lawyer Milloy, Patriots safety

|0> Heading into the AFC Championship Game, everybody thought we were lucky because of the overturned call against Oakland. We saw it differently; it was a turning point and rejuvenated our season. **1|0> Pittsburgh had a new stadium,** the number one defense and was a hostile, negative environment for us. We went into that stadium against all odds. Nobody believed in us, but us. **2|0> That particular week,** Coach Belichick sent Tom Brady and I to Pittsburgh a day early for the AFC Championship press conference. All the questions directed at us – players who prepared all week and were actually going out on the field to play – were about whether we thought we had "a chance" to win. That was a slap in our face. I had to count to 10 because I was so furious. I made a joke out of it, but I didn't really think it was funny. **3|0> Pittsburgh is similar to Boston** in that fans there love their sports and that was obvious from the time we arrived. They knew we were coming and everyone was dressed in black and gold. I went to IHOP with Ty Law's mother and her friend, who are from the area. They weren't totally decked out in Patriots stuff, but had some on and when they joined the buffet line, the restaurant manager joked with them about Steeler power. **4|0> He then came to our table with our waitress and put down a bottle of Heinz ketchup –** Pittsburgh is world headquarters for that company and the Steelers play in Heinz Field – and black-and-gold cookies. I didn't know what they had talked about at the buffet, and whether or not they knew who I was. I already had my game face on and glared at the waitress. **5|0> She said, "We decided to share a little black-and-gold** with you since this is the last decent meal you'll have before we crush you tomorrow." It was all in good fun, but I was furious. Ty's mom could see it in my face and she asked the manager if he knew who I was. "No. Who is he?" She told them, and the lady blushed. I asked her to remove the stuff from our table. **6|0> I wasn't comfortable until I heard the sirens guiding the buses with the rest of the team** on board into the city. I didn't want to stay Friday night in the first place; I told Tom that I wanted to fly back and return to Pittsburgh with the team, but he talked me out of it because it meant two more flights before a big game. **7|0> We went to dinner that night and talked.** I've been in the league for a while and I wanted to see what made him click, where his head was. We discussed what was at stake, but mostly about why we were enjoying success. He was very interested in what I had to say and I realized that he was very focused. It wasn't about fame or money for Tom; like me, he has passion for this game. **8|0> Tom described himself as the type of player who hasn't always been the fastest or strongest,** but whose competitive nature always had him racing the fastest player on the block until he beat him. **9|0> I joked with him that after about the 30th time,** the guy probably let him win so he could go home for supper. But that's his mentality and I realized we had a lot in common. As long as I approach the game and lead that way, he does it on the other side of the ball, and we're on the same team, our team will be solid for a while. **10|0> That competitive approach** filters through a team when its leaders bring it into a huddle and that definitely happened with this club. With it comes a certain level of confidence, and those two ingredients – along with plenty of motivation – helped us beat the Steelers that weekend and go on to win the Super Bowl.

THE WILD POST-GAME CELEBRATION WAS UNDER WAY AND BLEDSOE WAS AT ITS HEART

Ahead by only one score, New England's offense needed to eat some clock, regardless of whether it scored again, and it did just that with a 10-play possession that ended in a punt. The Patriots did not score, but they had intercepted Pittsburgh's momentum.

Bledsoe, who cooled off after his initial onslaught, hit his most important passes of the second half with his team backed against the wall, deep in its own end with the crowd noise at deafening decibel levels. First he hit tight end Jermaine Wiggins for four yards on third-and-3 from the 16. Then, facing third-and-11 from his own 19 with 5:58 to go, Bledsoe delivered his prettiest pass of the day, dropping an 18-yard rainbow over linebacker Mike Jones' outstretched hands into Brown's for a first down to the 37.

Pittsburgh did regain possession of the football, but the shiny new stadium clock was now an enemy. Pressed from all quarters, Stewart tossed back-to-back interceptions to Tebucky Jones and Milloy, underthrowing Hines Ward on the first, and overthrowing Plaxico Burress on the game-ender.

When Bledsoe took a knee to end the game and send the Patriots to their third Super Bowl in franchise history, tears streamed down his face – tears of joy and perhaps redemption. Bledsoe had proved his mettle on the grand stage and once again felt like a Patriot.

"It was a little overwhelming at the end," Bledsoe admitted. "The team has done great all year, but for me personally it's been a very long year."

THE PATRIOTS FINALLY

ABOVE ROBERT KRAFT CELEBRATES HIS SECOND AFC CHAMPIONSHIP AS PATRIOTS OWNER WITH HIS TWO PRO BOWL QUARTERBACKS **LEFT TO RIGHT** YET ANOTHER DOUSING FOR HEAD COACH BILL BELICHICK

The wild post-game celebration was under way and Bledsoe was at its heart.

"We've been feeling Drew's pain all year," Milloy said. "We respected the way Drew handled the situation; he didn't make it a distraction. I don't think any other team could say it has two Pro Bowl quarterbacks."

The Lamar Hunt Trophy awarded to the AFC Champion was headed to New England for the second time in six years, and owner Robert Kraft accepted it, remarking on the irony of the team's surname in the process. "In the year 2002, we think it's great for a team named 'Patriots' to be going into the greatest game in the country," he said.

As the Patriots cleaned out their Heinz Field lockers, their Super Bowl itinerary still unannounced, Milloy figured he didn't need to wait. "I need to catch one of the Steelers going out the door so I can get his room in New Orleans," he fired sarcastically, knowing Pittsburgh's bags were already packed.

A shock to many, the Patriots were headed to the Crescent City for a third shot at world glory. The juggernaut St. Louis Rams, the last team to defeat the Patriots in 2001, would represent the final hurdle.

The Patriots finally had some respect.

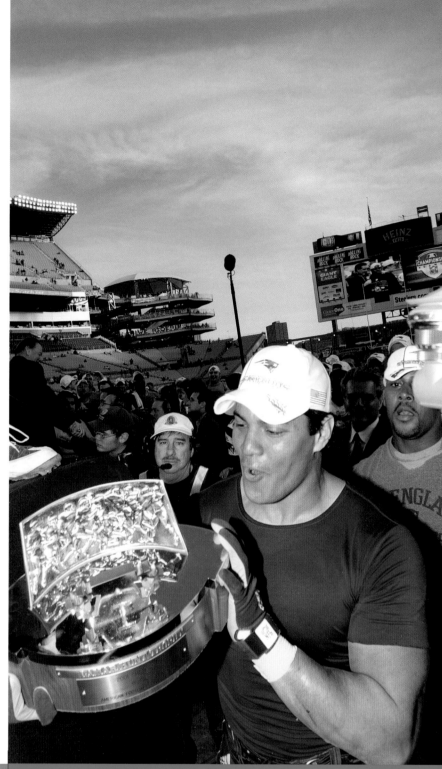

HAD SOME RESPECT

ABOVE RIGHT TEDY BRUSCHI HAS HIS TURN WITH THE PRIZE **LEFT TO RIGHT** LAWYER MILLOY, DAMIEN WOODY HOLDS UP THE HARDWARE, BLEDSOE, PATRIOTS FANS IN PITTSBURGH, BLEDSOE IN AN EMOTIONAL POST-GAME INTERVIEW

0> *The Big Easy and the New England Patriots* fostered a love-hate relationship long before the Patriots secured their first-ever world championship in New Orleans' Louisiana Superdome. **1|0>** **The first two New Orleans trips** to battle for league supremacy were anything but super. **2|0>** **The 1985 Patriots magical run** through the playoffs ended with a crushing Super Bowl XX defeat to one of the most impressive champions in history. Mike Ditka's Chicago Bears lost only one game all season and the Patriots proved no match for a dominating "46" defense anchored by Mike Singletary – among the best of all time. **3|0>** **The 46-10 drubbing** didn't erase the miraculous way in which the Patriots arrived in the championship or the euphoria that latched on for the ride. Improbable playoff road wins over the Jets, Raiders and Dolphins, the latter marking the first Patriots win in the Orange Bowl in 18 years, launched New England into a frenzy that had even the most cynical fan believing that Lady Destiny would provide the needed final nudge. New England was suddenly agog with excitement as Raymond Berry led his Patriots to its first Battle of New Orleans. But the Monsters of the Midway sucked the joy out of every town from Bangor to Boston and Hartford to Harwich. **4|0>** **Eleven years later in 1996,** with the prolific Drew Bledsoe at the helm and the indomitable Bill Parcells in full control of the bridge, the Patriots sailed back to the Crescent City for another chance at the ultimate prize. **5|0>** **Facing the NFC's most dominating team** in the Green Bay Packers, the Patriots had more realistic championship aspirations even if fans downplayed their optimism for fear of emotional letdown. When New England turned a 10-0 deficit into a 14-10 lead, the game was on and hope rekindled. **6|0>** **But the Packers posted the next 17 points** and a Patriots comeback was thwarted when Desmond Howard dashed through the Patriots coverage for a 99-yard, game-clinching touchdown and a 35-21 Packers victory. **7|0>** **And here they were again in the Crescent City,** facing an overwhelming favorite from the NFC. Same scenario, same setting, but a vastly different Patriots team.

IMAGES FROM
SUPER BOWLS
PAST IN NEW
ORLEANS –
XX VS. CHICAGO
AND XXXI VS.
GREEN BAY

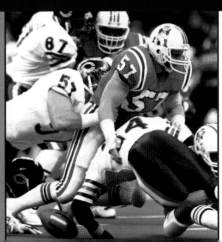

CHAPTER 11

INTRODUCING THE PATRIOTS

The 2001 New England Patriots

epitomized coach Bill Belichick's

football philosophy. Play tough.

Play smart. Play under control.

And the most important maxim

of all: Play as a team.

THE LOUISIANA SUPERDOME, SITE OF THE THREE NEW ENGLAND SUPER BOWL APPEARANCES

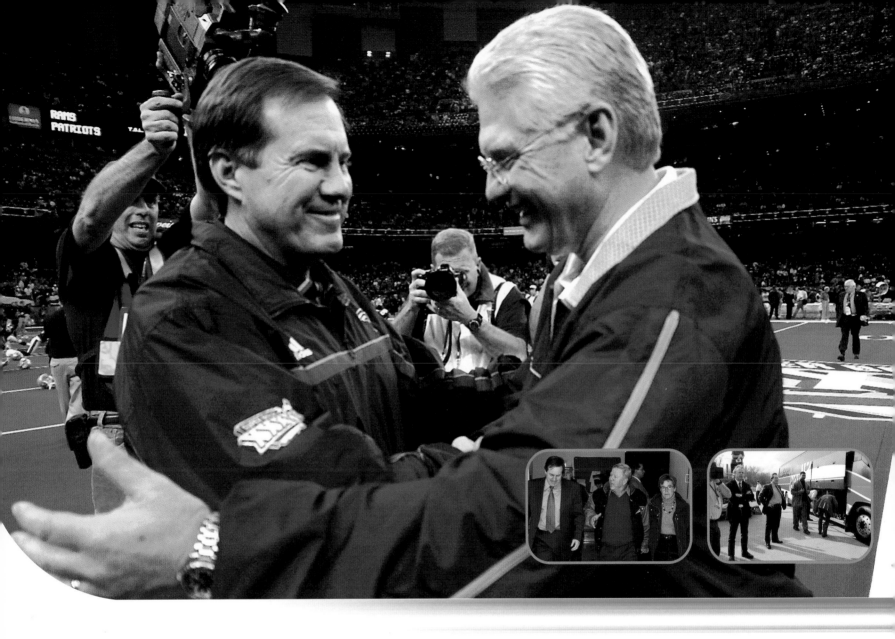

"I'M TRYING TO COACH A FOOTBALL TEAM AND PREPARE

"There is an old saying that the strength of the wolf is the pack, and I think there is a lot of truth to that. On a football team it's not the strength of the individual players, but the strength of the unit, and how everyone functions together." – Bill Belichick

Belichick was especially gracious during the week in the Big Easy. "It's not about vindication," he said during Super Bowl media day. "As a coach you go out every week and put your best out there to try to win the game. If you've done a good job, you feel good about it."

Despite his modesty, the 2001 season also was about Belichick proving he could win as an NFL head coach. His maturity and growth in that capacity shone through during the week's festivities as the once cold, occasionally confrontational coach stood at ease in the national spotlight, smiling, joking, and even admitting to past mistakes.

To be sure, charisma didn't exactly flow from his words nor ooze from his body language, but he belonged on this big stage.

ABOVE BILL BELICHICK AND MIKE MARTZ REPRESENT TWO OF THE BEST FOOTBALL MINDS IN THE BUSINESS

"I feel like I am still who I am for better or worse, whatever that is," he said unapologetically. "I'm trying to coach a football team and prepare it to win. That's my job."

It was a job Bill Belichick mastered in 2001 as he calmly guided a worst-to-first turnaround that had the Patriots playing for a world championship. His place was secure next to Raymond Berry and Bill Parcells as the only Patriots head coaches to reach the Super Bowl, but he could surpass them as the only man to finish the job.

T TO WIN. THAT'S MY JOB"
— BILL BELICHICK

As it turned out, New Orleans would be the Patriots Super Bowl home away from home. The team's first two title challenges ended in sound defeat at the Louisiana Superdome and now New England was back in the Big Easy hoping the third time would be the charm. The Crescent City greeted the Patriots warmly as they landed there 17 hours after arriving home from their AFC Championship triumph amidst throngs of supporters who braved the raw cold at Foxboro Stadium to greet their Super Bowl-bound heroes.

The players stepped off the plane with their camcorders rolling as a small jazz band and a light media contingent welcomed them to the host city. Upon arrival at team headquarters, the venerable Fairmont Hotel on the edge of the city's famed French Quarter and Bourbon Street, Belichick briefed the media for the first time.

The pressing questions revolved around his quarterbacks. Who would start the Super Bowl? Drew Bledsoe off his AFC Championship game relief win or Tom Brady, the starter since Week Three, but the one hobbled with a sprained ankle? Belichick was noncommittal, promising an answer after the team's Wednesday practice.

"I'm not trying to keep anything from you," Belichick said some 24 hours after his team's win over the Steelers. "It's too early. You can ask me in 50 different ways and I'll say the same thing: I'll answer it on Wednesday." True to his word, on Wednesday night the coach announced that Brady would start Super Bowl XXXVI.

While most media chatter focused on the Rams talent and superiority (one scribe said tongue-in-cheek that the Rams would win 73-0), their improved defense and their track team speed, the Patriots immersed themselves in stopping St. Louis' multifaceted attack through diligent preparation – Belichick's staple.

The impending duel between Belichick and St. Louis Head Coach Mike Martz was even more intriguing than Belichick versus Oakland's Jon Gruden had been two weeks before. These were two master football innovators, X and O gurus. The Rams, taking Martz's cue, repeated their season-long mantra that they could only lose by beating themselves. They were quick to point out that they do what they do regardless of the opponent.

181

THE MEDIA HORDE ON HAND
FOR SUPER BOWL WEEK
IS UNLIKE ANY OTHER

AND THAT IS NEVER MORE OBVIOUS

SCENES FROM MEDIA DAY **LEFT TO RIGHT** RICHARD SEYMOUR, PATRICK PASS AND MIKE VRABEL CONDUCT THEIR OWN INTERVIEW, BELICHIC

That turned out to be a glaring blunder against the Patriots. Belichick lives to negate the opposition's strength, and the Rams were about to learn that arrogantly "doing what we do" would cost them a championship, as the Patriots attacked their heart until their title aspirations flat-lined.

While it is fashionable to call Belichick a defensive genius, the jury had still been out on his ability to motivate when Kraft hired him two years before. Motivation and manipulation are occasionally synonymous, and with one game remaining Belichick had his players convinced that they could "shock the world," simply by playing Patriots football.

"We have to play a near-perfect game to beat them," Milloy conceded. "We have to slow them down and let them know they are in a war. They don't like to be hit and that's evident on game film. We have very few edges, if any, but that's definitely one of the edges we're looking at. We have to be physical with this group."

New England's plan was clear. Hit the Rams at every turn. Hit NFL MVP Marshall Faulk on every snap. Punish their speedy receivers. Challenge them and disrupt their timing; make quarterback Kurt Warner hold the ball until the rusher arrives to crush him.

The defensive plan was brilliant and its execution near perfect. The offense, after pounding away with running back Antowain Smith and his 18 carries for 92 yards, eventually called on Brady.

Despite 13 wins in 16 outings, including an eight-game winning streak, Brady had never really convinced his doubters. While Bledsoe breathed down his neck, the former Wolverine shielded himself from distractions and made plays whenever his team needed them.

In October, doubters wondered how he would respond to a four-interception fourth quarter against Denver. So he threw three touchdowns without a turnover the following week in Atlanta. In November, they wondered how he would fare with Bledsoe back and the pressure to perform increasing. He responded with four touchdown passes against the Saints.

Tom Brady didn't exactly set the football world ablaze through December as his team rolled inexorably onward. The critics were relentless; now they wondered how the Californian would perform under the strain of the NFL playoffs.

Once again, he responded: rallying the Patriots back from a 13-3 fourth quarter deficit against the Raiders by completing nine straight passes on one touchdown drive and eight straight in an overtime, game-winning march.

Still they wondered.

Now it was the Super Bowl, yet Brady lay sleeping in the locker room during the lengthy pre-game show.

THAN DURING TUESDAY MEDIA DAY

A SAMPLING OF THE MEDIA HORDE, LAWYER MILLOY, LAW, BROWN, MILLOY AND BRADY MUG FOR THE CAMERAS, PRACTICE AT TULANE UNIVERSITY

THE PATRIOTS EMERGED AS ONE, INTRODUCED SIMPLY AS THE "AFC CHAMPION NEW ENGLAND PATRIOTS"

The Patriots were prepared for the St. Louis Rams; their week's work provided a confidence level that allowed Brady to take a quick snooze without having to nervously cram at the last minute for the toughest football test of his life. Minutes later, he was enthusiastically crashing into a mosh pit of teammates, bumping shoulders and butting heads in the tunnel prior to the player introductions. And then the Patriots emerged as one, introduced simply as the "AFC Champion New England Patriots."

For all the build-up, the game began slowly.

The Rams led 3-0 midway through the second quarter before the Patriots took advantage of the game's first key turnover. St. Louis right tackle Rod Jones missed a blocking assignment, allowing linebacker Mike Vrabel a clear path to Warner, who tried in vain to brace himself as he threw errantly into Law's arms. With nothing but open field ahead of him, the Patriots cornerback raced to the end zone for the game's first touchdown and a 7-3 Patriots lead.

New England was going toe-to-toe with the consensus champion with no sign of backing down.

A second turnover for the Rams proved costly as well when their trademark two-minute offense uncharacteristically failed them. Warner fired a 15-yard pass down the middle to Ricky Proehl. As Proehl lunged forward to the turf to avoid contact, Patriots defensive back Antwan Harris drilled him on the football, forcing it loose. Terrell Buckley scooped up the bouncing ball and returned it to the Rams 40 with 1:31 remaining in the half.

and rattled, as New England pushed his team around, but St. Louis still had 15 minutes left. The Rams marched 74 yards to open the final quarter and faced a critical fourth-and-goal situation from the Patriots 3-yard line with 10:21 to go. Warner dropped back to pass, but with no one open, scrambled to his right only to be chased down by linebacker Roman Phifer, who dislodged the ball on the three. There, Tebucky Jones grabbed it and sprinted 97 yards for a touchdown.

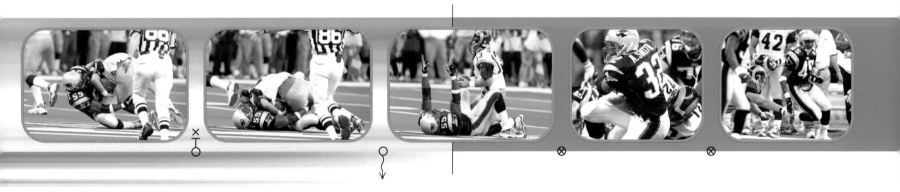

Five plays later, David Patten leaped high to haul in an 8-yard touchdown pass in the corner of the end zone for a 14-3 Patriots half-time lead that prompted radio announcer Howard David to wonder aloud, "Can you believe what is happening here in New Orleans?"

The Patriots always believed, and their physical style caused a third St. Louis turnover late in the third quarter when Otis Smith bumped Torry Holt off his route and intercepted Warner's throw, setting up Adam Vinatieri's first field goal, a 37-yarder that made it 17-3 Patriots through three quarters.

No team had kept the clamps on the Rams high-octane offense all season, but the Patriots limited it to three points through 45 minutes of football. Warner appeared confused

Almost unnoticed on the opposite side of the field, however, a solitary yellow penalty flag lay in the end zone. The call was defensive holding and the culprit was Willie McGinest, who had hugged Faulk on his way out of the backfield. Two plays later, Warner ran up the middle for a 2-yard touchdown to make it 17-10. A familiar sinking feeling began to envelop Patriots Nation.

The 14-point swing was reminiscent of a similar situation in the teams' first meeting when Smith's fumble inside the Rams 5-yard line had been converted into a touchdown just before half-time.

185

By Ron Jaworski, ESPN football analyst

0> **Bill Belichick did a magnificent job throughout the season,** but what made his Super Bowl coaching job special for me was the respect I have for Mike Martz and what he can do to a defense – how he can break it down and create favorable personnel match-ups. **10>** **In the Super Bowl,** Bill dictated the match-ups, causing confusion and doing all the things necessary to force a high-octane offense out of sync. It wasn't only from an Xs-and-Os standpoint; it was Bill's psychological approach as well. He understood that Mike Martz would almost exclusively focus on the passing game and almost forget about Marshall Faulk, and it played out that way. It was like Bill was in Mike's head and structured his defense accordingly. **20>** **In the game, the Patriots used five defensive backs** on 23 snaps, six defensive backs on another 23 snaps, and seven defensive backs on seven snaps. Overall, the Patriots had five or more defensive backs on the field 74 percent of the time and invited the Rams to run the football. You have to run at defensive backs and get those big bodies out knocking down those small guys. Martz refused to be aggressive with Faulk and the running game, which is why Bill won the mind game as well. **30>** **The physical approach the Patriots took** was unique. Normally when you are breaking down the passing game from a physical perspective, you think about getting hits on the quarterback. The Patriots focused their physical play on Faulk and the wide receivers rather than on Kurt Warner. They did an incredible job of chipping Faulk as he came out of the backfield. In fact, guys like Roman Phifer and Willie McGinest wouldn't even rush Warner, but instead chased and hit Faulk. They really broke down the timing and rhythm of the Rams explosive passing attack by being physical with the receivers. **40>** **Martz does a great job creating favorable match-ups** and there was one play in the game where, through formation variation and motion, Martz created the match-up he wanted – Phifer on Torry Holt. Anyone would take Holt in that match-up, but Phifer did a great job of drilling Holt at the line of scrimmage and didn't allow a clean release, and Holt never got off the ball. The physical play negated the Rams quickness and speed, and a match-up that should have favored the Rams favored the Patriots instead. **50>** **Bill and Romeo Crennel** mixed things up so well. Ty Law's interception was a terrific example of that. It came on the Rams 27th offensive play in the game and was the first time the Patriots were in their five down linemen front. It caused a blocking mistake and allowed Mike Vrabel to come clean after the quarterback, which led to a defensive touchdown. The timing was exquisite. The Rams did some things offensively because they are that good and the most formidable offense the NFL's ever seen, but the Patriots defense was so well coached and prepared. **60>** **Offensively, many teams change their offense** against the Rams, anticipating a high-scoring game, but Charlie Weis stayed with what he did all year long. They played within themselves. They had the mandate to control and take care of the football and be physical. **70>** **Going into the game,** I thought Troy Brown was the Pats only big-time playmaker and they had to get him involved. So on the first play, they spread the field and got the ball to Troy, making sure the Rams were thinking about him. Then they came back with a power running game and moved the ball well on the ground. **80>** **New England did a great job in running out of their two-tight end formation,** using it on 23 of 54 snaps or 42 percent of the time. I'm a big believer in first down and they were effective out of that formation and controlled first down. Antowain Smith ran six times for 47 yards on first down, dictating the tempo of the game. **90>** **As I said, it was the best coaching job I've ever seen** and it came in the biggest game

LEARNING FROM EXPERIENCE

By Romeo Crennel, Patriots defensive coordinator

|0> **When we played St. Louis the first time,** our goal defensively was to present multiple fronts and coverages to disrupt their passing game. This mix of coverages included applying varied types of pressure. While we did cause them some trouble, they were definitely able to handle the different looks and the various pressures we applied. Rams quarterback Kurt Warner did a good job of running their offense and controlling our multiple defenses.

1|0> **The second time around,** our goal was the same – disrupt their passing game. To do that, we played to the strengths of our players. We are a physical and aggressive team and we wanted to use these strengths to our advantage. By hitting the receivers and breaking the pocket with a four-man rush, we were able to disrupt the Rams offense. The coverage mix featured a little more zone defense and in this game it worked for us. We gave up fewer passing yards than in the first game and we didn't allow any big plays until late in the game. 2|0> **Overall, our players played hard in both games.** We came up a touchdown short in the first game, but that allowed us to experience the Rams speed and ability first-hand, and that made us feel we could compete with them. When we got our second chance, it was our physical and aggressive style that allowed us to take an early lead and win the game.

> A LITTLE TINKERING

PLAY NAME: F RIGHT FING 50 OUT GO Z SLANT

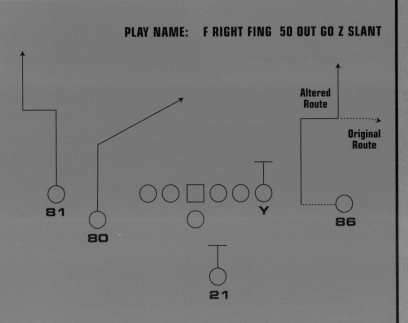

Altered Route

Original Route

81

80

Y

86

21

Friday night before Super Bowl XXXVI, offensive coordinator Charlie Weis and Bill Belichick decided to alter one of their red zone pass plays and the result was a critical touchdown just before half-time. On the play diagrammed, wide receiver David Patten was originally supposed to run an "out" pattern, but Weis and Belichick correctly concluded that Rams cornerback Dexter McCleon would bite on the "out" so they changed Patten's route to an "out-and-up." The Patriots never practiced the play before the Super Bowl as the coaches simply passed along the change verbally. It was executed to perfection in the Super Bowl – another feather in the cap of the innovative Weis and the eternally prepared Belichick. It provided further proof of the team's focus and ability to execute. Tom Brady to Patten for an 8-yard touchdown gave New England a 14-3 half-time lead.

The Patriots clung to their fragile 7-point lead until St. Louis flexed its muscles, effortlessly driving 55 yards in three plays and 21 seconds to tie the score on a 26-yard Warner-to-Proehl strike. The Patriots defense was out of gas.

Finally, here came the expected seltzer-in-your-pants and pie-in-the-face after months of daring to finally believe. Here came the Punch Line: the typical New England collapse. Faces in hands, Patriots fans sat in silent shock, their team reverting to form. Would McGinest's holding penalty rival Bill Buckner's error in New England sports lore? The Patriots had dominated for 45 minutes and now sat tied, 17-17, with 1:21 to go and the ball on their own 17-yard line with no timeouts.

The most optimistic scenario now had the Pats holding off the Rams until overtime, and then maybe pulling out some miracle in the fifth quarter. One loud proponent of this strategy was FOX Sports color man John Madden, and he expounded it to an audience of millions.

On the sideline, however, Bill Belichick, the dour Bill Belichick, the defensive guru Bill Belichick, had an audience of only one. He turned to Tom Brady and quietly told him to go out and win it. Now. Out trotted the rookie signal caller, who was 11-of-19 for only 92 yards in the game's first 58:39.

ABOVE RIGHT   RICHARD SEYMOUR GETS INTO THE RAMS BACKFIELD   LEFT TO RIGHT   MARSHALL FAULK SURROUNDED, SEYMOUR, BOBBY HAMILTON, MCGINEST, LAW AND MILLOY CELEBRATE LAW'S INTERCEPTION RETURN

OF THE INDIVIDUAL PLAYERS,
AND HOW EVERYONE FUNCTIONS TOGETHER"

—BILL BELICHICK

|0> **Performance under fire defines a quarterback.** While Tom Brady's critics minimized his stats from the day he took over the offense, the cucumber-cool youngster surpassed all previous New England passers in guiding the Patriots to a first Super Bowl title, thanks in large part to his play when outcomes hung in the balance. 1|0> **Heading into the playoffs,** Brady's inexperience on the big stage was a hot topic in New England, but he responded in his first play-off game against Oakland with two fourth-quarter scoring drives, the second in the pressure-packed hurry-up offense to tie the game. He then added another in overtime to send the Patriots to Pittsburgh for the AFC Championship. 2|0> **On the grandest of all stages,** in the final 1:21 of Super Bowl XXXVI without a timeout and the ball positioned at his own 17, Brady again displayed poise under pressure, guiding the Patriots 53 yards in eight plays to set up Adam Vinatieri's Super Bowl winning kick. 3|0> **"He just said, 'here we go,' "** wide receiver David Patten recalled. "He said we had to go down and win the game here. He has such a tremendous amount of confidence and it revs us up. If you look in his eyes and hear him talk, you think, 'We have to go out and get it done for this kid.'" 4|0> **The Patriots emphasize the team aspect of their success** and on the Super Bowl's final march it was more than just Brady who stepped up. Still, he was the quarterback and the decision-maker who has the ball in his hands on every snap. 5|0> **"The pass routes made the difference,** but Brady made the throws," said St. Louis linebacker London Fletcher. "He also made the right decisions." Brady began the drive by eluding backside pressure from Leonard Little, who swiped at the ball, and dumping off to J.R. Redmond for five yards. With the clock the enemy, Brady hurried his team to the line of scrimmage and again checked down to Redmond for eight yards and a first down at the 30-yard line, where he spiked the ball to stop the clock with 41 seconds on the clock. 6|0> **Brady swung the ball back to Redmond** on the fourth play of the drive, but the second-year running back had some room to run this time and avoided a tackler long enough to squirt out of bounds to stop the clock with 33 seconds left, after an 11-yard gain. If Redmond doesn't reach the sideline, the drive is over. 7|0> **Brady correctly read a safety blitz** and scrambled to his right away from Adam Archuleta to fire the ball into the Rams sideline, avoiding an intentional grounding penalty by escaping the tackle box and stopping the clock, on a play that took four seconds. 8|0> **The next play was the biggest of the drive** with Troy Brown finding a seam in the zone on a play called "64 Max All-In", where the receivers run in-cuts at different depths and the offensive line works to give the quarterback maximum protection. Brady stepped up and drilled a laser beam to Brown, who caught it and ran out of bounds at the Rams 36-yard line for a 23-yard gain to stop the clock at 21 seconds. 9|0> **"Tom did a great job of moving us down the field,** hitting the open guys, checkdowns, whatever. The last drive was tremendous for him," Brown said. Brady then threw a short 6-yard pass to tight end Jermaine Wiggins at the St. Louis 30 and then calmly brought his team to the line of scrimmage and spiked the ball to stop the clock at :07. His work done, Brady turned the game over to Adam Vinatieri, who delivered the knockout blow. 100> **"It was just awesome,"** Brady said in celebration. "Everybody got it done. Troy Brown made a big catch, J.R. Redmond, Adam Vinatieri – everybody. It's the way this team has responded all year when its back is against the wall." 110> **"It was a well executed two-minute drive,"** said head coach Bill

THE BUZZ RESUMED IN THE STANDS AS MORE THAN 70,000 SPECTATORS REALIZED A PATRIOTS CHAMPIONSHIP WAS WITHIN REACH

As it turned out, 81 seconds was plenty of time. The championship drive began with three checkdowns to J.R. Redmond, who made a marvelous play to squeeze out of bounds on the third to stop the clock with 33 seconds left and the ball at the Patriots 41.

Brady then fired one into the Rams bench to escape a blitz before connecting with Troy Brown over the middle for 23 yards. Brown's sprint out of bounds at the St. Louis 36 with 21 seconds left saved the drive.

The buzz resumed in the stands as more than 70,000 spectators realized a Patriots championship was within reach. St. Louis fans, whose hopes had soared earlier in the fourth quarter as their team mounted a comeback, were in anguish. They had heard about the no-nerves New England kicker and all eyes were on the Patriots sideline where the player with the big No. 4 on his jersey was casually swatting balls into a practice net.

His teammates, watching surreptitiously, knew what they had in the talented foot of the free agent from South Dakota State. Since signing on as a free agent in 1996, Vinatieri had recorded 100 points in each of his first six seasons. Even more remarkable was his family tree; he is a cousin to daredevil Evel Knievel, and the great, great-grandson of Felix Vinatieri, General George Armstrong Custer's bandmaster.

The resuscitated New England region was on its collective feet, hope rekindled, hearts pounding; the Pats fans in the Superdome clapped and screamed.

Joy, anxiety, hope and even more anxiety roiled around New England as Patriots Nation watched Brady hit tight end Jermaine Wiggins for six more yards and then calmly step up and spike the ball with seven ticks on the clock and the ball on the Rams 30.

Vinatieri's amazing right leg had prolonged the season with a 45-yarder through a blizzard in Foxboro. He now stood 48 yards away from the uprights, inside ideal dome conditions. He had never missed a dome field goal in his career. Norwood's miss on the final play of Super Bowl XXV clinched a victory for the New York Giants over the Bills, a play still recalled with anguish in Buffalo. As the fuse burned down, Vinatieri was about to become a hero or goat.

THE IMPOSSIBLE, THE INCREDIBLE, THE UNTHINKABLE,

THE (FILL IN YOUR OWN SUPERLATIVE) HAD HAPPENED

The dynamite's fuse was ignited and New England held its breath knowing that the slightest tremor could prevent it from reaching its destination, Dome or no Dome. New England fans seemed immersed in prayer as past failings danced in their heads.

Vinatieri trotted out alongside long snapper Lonie Paxton and holder Ken Walter, who at this moment were as vital to the cause as the kicker himself. The flame flickered ever closer as Walter planted his left knee on the right hash mark at the 38 and held up his right hand, ready to receive the snap.

"Is it Adam Vinatieri or Scott Norwood?" Howard David asked rhetorically.

The snap, the hold, the kick: Paxton to Walter to Vinatieri's toe... all perfect! The flame sparkled to its end. The kicking leg slashed forward, the ball sailed high and true in a winning arc, and Vinatieri's clenched fists thrust upward as he leaped off the turf and watched the ball split the uprights as the clock struck 00:00.

New England exploded into a Fourth of July-type fireworks celebration. The lifelong always-a-bridesmaid-never-a-bride stigma was eradicated in an instant. The impossible, the incredible, the unthinkable, the (fill in your own superlative here) had happened.

ADAM VINATIERI'S FOOT KICKED OFF THE CELEBRATION FOR THE PATRIOTS AND THEIR FANS

THE VINCE LOMBARDI TROPHY WAS

ABOVE THE VINCE LOMBARDI TROPHY HELD HIGH **LEFT TO RIGHT** THE SUPERDOME SCOREBOARD TELLS THE STORY WHILE IN THE OWNER'S BOX, JONATHAN AND ROBERT KRAFT REALIZE THEY OWN THE WORLD CHAMPION FOOTBALL TEAM

The Patriots sideline erupted as players sprinted to mob the hero kicker. New England was one huge living room, where thousands reacted simultaneously and similarly, tears of joy mingling with jubilant hugs and screams. In one spectacular, glorious moment, all of New England instinctively knew the meaning of a Greek word: Euphoria!

For the first time in their 42-year existence, the New England Patriots were world champions, 20-17 winners over the heavily favored St. Louis Rams. The Vince Lombardi Trophy was finally coming to New England.

The Patriots had their respect; they earned it by controlling the championship game the way winning teams do. They didn't gloat, but they had a point to make in the post-game interviews.

"If we listened to the experts, we shouldn't have even bothered showing up," Willie McGinest said. "If you can't respect us now, you should quit your job and get into some other walk of life. We controlled this game from start to finish. This was no upset. They never had control of the game."

INALLY COMING TO NEW ENGLAND

197

ABOVE RIGHT BELICHICK AND HIS PERSONNEL DIRECTOR SCOTT PIOLI
LEFT TO RIGHT BRUSCHI, MCGINEST AND SEYMOUR, THE CONFETTI RAINS OVER THE PATRIOTS

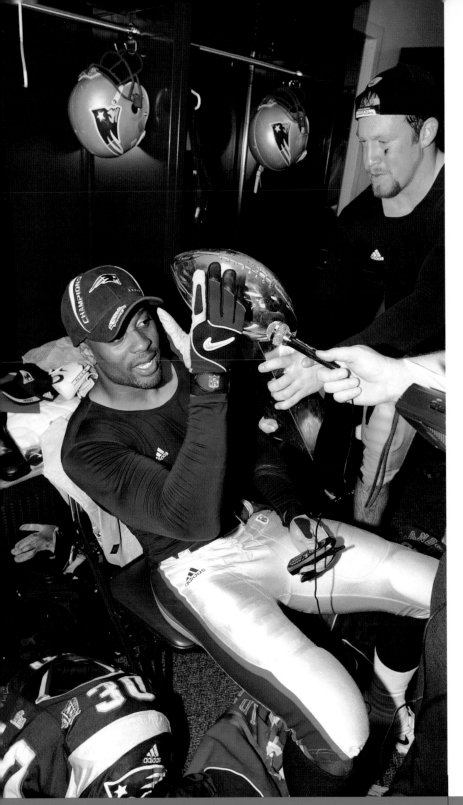

"Our game is force," linebacker Tedy Bruschi added. "Today finesse met force and something had to give. That was the theme all week. We're a team that's physical, that likes to hit people, that likes to knock them down and stand over them, and they're a team that likes to zig and zag. Today force won."

Tom Brady, the game's MVP, shared the glory. "I can't say enough about this team. Whenever our backs are against the wall, the way we respond under pressure is unbelievable. I can't believe we're world champs."

Super Bowl XXXVI was the first ever to end on the game's final play, and its drama was unrivaled. The Patriots walked onto the field at the Louisiana Superdome as a team, and fought their way off through the roiling crowds, cameras and mountains of confetti, as a team of champions. They emerged after 60 minutes of pigskin war, after the most brilliant hour of football in the franchise's history. They proved that pure talent doesn't always win over pure will, and that with unity much can be accomplished.

"The players have done a tremendous job of being unselfish and being a team," Belichick said. "That's what we were out there today. That's why we won; because we played as a team."

That team, the 2001 New England Patriots, is quite possibly the greatest sports champion in New England's rich history.

ABOVE LEFT LARRY IZZO HANDS OFF THE HARDWARE TO FELLOW SPECIAL TEAM STALWART JE'ROD CHERRY LEFT TO RIGHT LONIE PAXTON, BELICHICK, CHARLIE WEIS

ABOVE MARC EDWARDS SPREADS THE NEWS LEFT TO RIGHT BLEDSOE AND SON STUART,
FOX COLOR MAN TERRY BRADSHAW WITH BRADY AND VINATIERI, ANTOWAIN SMITH

Congratulations
Super Bowl XXXVI
Champions

New England
PATRIOTS

THREE PARTIES AND A CHAMPIONSHIP

MORE THAN FOUR MONTHS LATER,

THE DECIBEL LEVEL HAD FINALLY

ABATED. CONVERSELY, PRIDE

OF ACCOMPLISHMENT HAD

GROWN EXPONENTIALLY.

THE PARADE THROUGH THE STREETS OF BOSTON   L TO R: ROBERT KRAFT, HIS GRANDSON HARRY, SCOTT PIOLI

The staff of the posh Boston Harbor Hotel pranced from table to table to present each of the Patriots with a gift box, and the expressions on the faces of the players told the story. Inside each one was the final piece of validation, something that would remain with them forever – their Super Bowl ring – and the building excitement virtually drowned out the words of Robert Kraft.

For 23 years, Kraft had journeyed to Foxboro Stadium as a season ticket holder with his four sons – Jonathan, Dan, Josh and David – to watch the New England Patriots. Through thick and thin, usually thin and thinner, the family persevered in their love affair with the Pats, never wavering and never losing hope.

This was also a family's validation.

Their proud owner stood before them and explained the significance and symbolism in the design of the rings, but the players' enthusiasm made his pitch as effective as a substitute teacher's. The owner talked about the 143 diamonds, red garnet and blue sapphire that comprised the team logo, the word "team" inscribed on the side along with player names and numbers.

"This ring is a symbol of 42 years of waiting to be a part of this," Kraft said. "Thanks for helping make our dream come true."

ABOVE LEFT THE NORMALLY QUIET TROY BROWN HAS SOMETHING TO SAY ON THIS DAY
LEFT TO RIGHT DAN AND ROBERT KRAFT; THREE GENERATIONS. **GROWNUPS, L TO R:** WENDY, DAN, DAVID, JOSH, ROBERT, MYRA, JONATHAN, PATTI. **KIDS, L TO R:** ALLISON, JESSICA, HARRY, SADIE; JONATHAN SHARES THE SPOILS WITH FANS

The post-Super Bowl reverie had known three distinct celebratory events. The first was the blur of partying, good old fashioned hooting and hollering that began with the final whistle at the Superdome and the presentation of the Lombardi Trophy. It then moved to the clubhouse and followed the players back to the Fairmont Hotel. Finally, the revelry continued onto the team charter home.

Several hangovers later, what the players remembered most about the partying was the sense of exhilaration and relief after a golden season finally resulted in a championship. This was emotional release on an altogether different level.

In a year when rampant patriotism spread through America as quickly as the tragic news of September 11, the New England Patriots fittingly captured the nation's heart with a special unity that led to ultimate victory. It was a win for the red, white and blue and for America's teamwork so prevalent

in New York City and Washington D.C. That fact was not lost on Kraft as he stood at the Louisiana Superdome 50-yard line and accepted the Vince Lombardi Trophy from NFL commissioner Paul Tagliabue, who called Super Bowl XXXVI "a game for the ages."

"The Kraft family is happy to be associated with coaches and team players who put team first, as the way they came out of the tunnel tonight; and in a way, the fact that our players and coaches, at this time in our country when people are banding together for a higher cause, can feel this special spirit of America, we're proud to be a symbol of that in some small way," said Robert Kraft.

"Spirituality, faith and democracy are the cornerstones of our country. We are all Patriots and tonight the Patriots are world champions."

MVT – MOST VALUABLE TEAM

Does the Cadillac Escalade EXT sport utility vehicle awarded to the Super Bowl MVP have seating for 53? It better. **Tom Brady graciously accepted** the luxury vehicle after copping the Pete Rozelle Trophy, but the youngest quarterback ever to win a Super Bowl was quick to point out, before jetting off to Disney World, that it was a shared award. **"There's a lot of guys who deserve that car,"** Brady said. "It's a team car now. Everyone is using it. The quarterback is only as good as the guys around him and I'm on a team with unbelievable talent." **Brady, 24, completed 16-of-27 passes for 145 yards** and one touchdown in the game, but saved his best moments for the clutch. He threw his only touchdown pass of the post-season in a hurry-up situation just before half-time, and then engineered the game winning drive in the final 81 seconds by completing 5-of-8 passes for 53 yards with no timeouts to set up Adam Vinatieri's game-winning kick. The men who walked into the Super Bowl as a team left as champions. **"We're not a group of individuals.** We're not running out one at a time. When we're running out, we're running out as a team and we're winning as a team and losing as a team. And that's why we won nine straight," Brady said after becoming the second youngest player to win the MVP award behind fellow Junipero Serra High School alum, and former Steelers receiver, Lynn Swann. **The ninth win, of course,** came Super Bowl Sunday. Playing what Bill Belichick called simply "Patriots football," New England smothered the Rams with physical play from gun to gun until a championship was in hand. It was such a team victory that the MVP voting was split among several players with the online fan tally swaying it in Brady's favor. **The young, enthusiastic offensive leader** had the perfect summary. "We've got an MVT – Most Valuable Team," he said. "They've done a great job of being unselfish and being a team," Bill Belichick added. "That's what they were out there today and that's the reason we won."

LEFT TO RIGHT
LAW AND JONES
LEAD TERRELL
BUCKLEY UPFIELD
AFTER HIS FUMBLE
RECOVERY, OTIS
SMITH WITH AN
INTERCEPTION,
BRADY SAVORS
THE MOMENT

"WE ARE ALL PATRIOTS AND TONIGHT THE PATRIOTS ARE WORLD CHAMPIONS"

— ROBERT KRAFT

With that, the luster of the Vince Lombardi trophy shone on New England as Kraft held it aloft, and the hometown celebration was officially under way.

The next celebration was the most important because it was shared with the fans. Back home, 1,500 miles away, New England had geared up for a Boston blowout like no other. A sea of a 1.5 million people lined the city streets and packed into City Hall Plaza, even climbing light poles and trees to get

a glimpse of the Patriots two days after their historic triumph – on winter's coldest day – and to be a part of the region's first professional sports championship since 1986, and perhaps its greatest ever.

Kraft said a few words and then turned over the microphone to head coach Bill Belichick, whose acquisition he called "the best deal I ever made." "We began this journey a long time ago in training camp," Belichick said.

209

ABOVE ROBERT AND JONATHAN KRAFT SURVEY THE 1.5 MILLION FANS LINING THE STREETS OF BOSTON LEFT TO RIGHT FANS CAME OUT IN DROVES TO CELEBRATE, JERMAINE WIGGINS AT BOSTON'S CITY HALL PLAZA, ASSISTANT HEAD COACH AND OFFENSIVE LINE COACH DANTE SCARNECCHIA

"IT'S OUR TIME. THEY DID IT.
CONGRATULATIONS CHAMPIONS"
— BILL BELICHICK

A CHAMPIONSHIP CAST

By Tedy Bruschi, Patriots linebacker

|0> **I must start by saying** that I have never been associated with so much open unselfishness in my sports career. I can't say how it came about or how this sort of dynamic happens, but once in a while it just does. We won Super Bowl XXXVI through total team play, and that's not a cliché. **|0>** **Our journey through the playoffs** was proof of it. We were down in the Raiders game and needed the offense to bring us back; Tom Brady completed nine straight passes in the snow because he had to, and Adam Vinatieri had to make the kick that won it for us. Then in Pittsburgh, defense and special teams won for us. In the Super Bowl, all aspects of the team contributed. We scored three offensive touchdowns in the playoffs and still went all the way because our entire team played well, not just a single part of it. **2|0>** **We had players return from injury** only to see their replacement continue playing because Bill Belichick stays with the hot hand. It started with Drew Bledsoe, but it happened at linebacker as well, where we had a revolving door in the middle with the injuries. I got hurt in Miami, Bryan Cox broke his leg in Denver and Ted Johnson got hurt the week of the Rams game. Each of us, at one time or another, was healthy but not playing as much as we wanted, and had to bite our tongues for the betterment of the team. **3|0>** **In my mind, our defense started coming together** in Atlanta in November. We played well against Buffalo, and then St. Louis came to town with the most potent offense in the NFL. With the exception of a few plays that Sunday night in Foxboro, we felt we should have won the game. **4|0>** **We went to a full-time 4-3 defense** for the Rams game. With Roman Phifer and Mike Vrabel playing so well on the outside and Bryan and Ted out, I moved to the middle. Until then I'd probably had a total of 10 plays at that position in my career. I had played a lot at weakside linebacker in a 4-3 front, which is an inside position with weak side responsibilities in pass coverage and run defense. The biggest transition to the middle linebacker spot was the strong side responsibilities. I winged it and relied on instinct at times. **5|0>** **We featured such a great cast of characters** with so many different personalities. One such player is Anthony Pleasant who, apart from his play on the field, you wouldn't know was in the locker room. He is a quiet, soft-spoken guy who is just vicious on the field. We had to have a presence in the middle and drafting Richard Seymour was huge. Once he was healthy and playing well, he made a million things easier for me in the middle because people had to focus on him and the disruption he could cause. **6|0>** **Roman Phifer was the best pickup we had.** He did everything. He played every down. He played in the nickel and dime and he played on the punt team. He was an unsung hero who didn't get a lot of credit. He has such an upbeat personality and is always cracking a joke to make guys laugh. His presence in the locker room and on the field was terrific. **7|0>** **On the other side, Mike Vrabel's play** was so consistent. The secondary was a tough, physical group. Each guy on our defense understood his role and trusted his teammates. That's why we were successful. We truly believed in one another and it was special to experience and be a part of a defense that evolved into a championship caliber group as ours did. **8|0>** **It all came down to unselfishness**

"It's been a long voyage and a long journey and we took the last step Sunday night. I feel like our journey is complete for this year.

"Before I turn this over to our captains, from whom we've had tremendous leadership all year, I'll just tell you that at 12 o'clock on game day before we went to the Superdome, I met with the team and the coaches and told them at that time that if we just follow the game plan and played our game and played Patriot football, that this would be our time. Right now for these players, it's our time. They did it. Congratulations Champions."

"At the beginning of the season, we started out a little slow," kicker Adam Vinatieri told the crowd, "and some of the reporters didn't think we had much of a chance. So we adopted a little motto and basically, if a reporter didn't believe in us, we would just say, 'Don't talk to me.'

"As the season went along, people said, 'Yeah they're doing better, but I don't think they got what it takes.' All we said is, 'Don't talk to me.'

"We kept going and won some more games and the Raiders came in and a lot of people didn't think we could win, but what?"

"HEY, WE'RE WORLD CHAMPIONS. DON'T TALK TO ME"
— ADAM VINATIERI

When there were games to be played, the 2001 Patriots had meticulously followed their coach's mantra. Say nothing when the time is not right.

But now, at the completion of a storybook Super Bowl championship run, the time to speak had come, and some of the pent-up emotion led to some choice words.

"They labeled us underdogs," team captain Lawyer Milloy screamed into the microphone, as the crowd roared.

"They gave us no respect. We got our respect now, right?"

"Don't talk to me!" the crowd roared.

"We got to Pittsburgh and we were nine-and-a-half-point underdogs and they were already printing the Super Bowl tickets," Vinatieri continued. "And what did we say?"

"Don't talk to me!"

"We go down to New Orleans and did anybody give us a chance? Nobody. And what did we say to them?"

"Don't talk to me!"

"Hey, we're world champions. Don't talk to me."

Troy Brown offered a less rhetorical summation.

"I've had the pleasure of watching this team become what I'm all about: quiet, unselfish, disciplined – that's what we've been about all year," Brown said.

"We kept our mouths shut and got the job done when nobody gave us a chance of doing it. We stuck together all year. I stood here last week [for a pre-Super Bowl rally] and told you that we were bringing the big one home. I never touched the AFC Championship trophy because number two is not a winner. I wanted to be a champion and I got my hands on the biggest prize of them all. Hey, we're not finished yet in Boston. I'm looking forward to doing this again next year."

On this day, February 5, 2002, the Patriots owned New England, and it was the "right season" to finally talk.

"This is your trophy," Milloy told the crowd. "We brought it home."

Now back at the Boston Harbor Hotel in June, the exhilaration was less vocal, but just as palpable, among the tinkling glasses and flatware.

Once given the go-ahead, the players opened their boxes the same way they earned what was inside – together – and the room was filled with laughter and joy of a special Christmas morning. In fact, that's how Debby Belichick, Bill's wife, described the scene as players hugged and waved their impressive rings at anyone who cared to look.

"This is something really special," wide receiver Troy Brown said. "You look at this thing and you realize why you do all that work. Winning championships is special and I hope we can get used to this kind of thing around here."

It's rare in the world of professional sports for an entire team to become truly excited about a particular event.

This was such a happening. As the classy mahogany boxes were opened – the glamour on full display – the organization took one final look back at what it had accomplished and once and for all turned the page on the magical 2001 Super Bowl championship season.

Mission accomplished.

THANKS FOR HELPING

"THIS RING IS A SYMBOL OF
FORTY-TWO YEARS OF WAITING
TO BE A PART OF THIS.

MAKE OUR DREAM COME TRUE"

— ROBERT KRAFT

ABOVE THE CHAMPIONSHIP RING   LEFT TO RIGHT THE WHITE HOUSE CEREMONY WITH PRESIDENT BUSH; PRESIDENT BUSH SIGNING
AUTOGRAPHS; WITH LAWYER MILLOY, DAVID, ROBERT, DAN AND JONATHAN KRAFT ON THE WHITE HOUSE LAWN

"WE TRULY BELIEVED IN ONE ANOTHER...
UNSELFISHNESS —

"IT ALL CAME DOWN TO

TOTAL TEAM — AND WE EPITOMIZED THAT"

— TEDY BRUSCHI

A LETTER FROM THE OWNER

So much has happened since I purchased the New England Patriots in January of 1994, but at the same time, it seems like yesterday. It's been one of the most exciting, joyous, anxious, frustrating and satisfying rides of my life all wrapped up into one. Something in '94 told me buying the Patriots was the right thing to do despite advice to the contrary and now, well, I'm glad I listened to that something – whatever it was.

For as long as there have been the Patriots, I have been a fan. The memories of watching games at Foxboro Stadium are something I treasure because it involves my biggest treasure, my family. My sons and I would cheer, argue and share in the frustration together with all other Patriots fans in what became a Sunday ritual. Still, it was tough watching someone else's champion pass us by each season.

This past season was the payoff for all of us. Those 42 years of waiting made this celebration that much sweeter. I'll never forget just two days after the Super Bowl standing on that stage in front of Boston City Hall and looking out over what I'm told was a 1.5 million Patriots fans. I felt so proud to be involved in something that gave so many people from so many walks of life so much happiness.

I'm also proud to have a team and coaching staff all dedicated to the same cause – winning, and giving our fans the absolute best product possible. You deserve it for all the support you've shown for over four decades.

Of course, success is fleeting in pro sports. You're only as good as your last performance and the task at hand for this organization is to remain champions.

What you are about to witness is a new era for the New England Patriots. We begin that journey in our new home, Gillette Stadium, as the best professional football team in the world. The sense of pride it evokes throughout our region and among Patriots fans wherever they live, is undeniable, and for good cause. Everyone who calls themselves Patriots fans should feel a strong sense of accomplishment knowing they had a large hand in making all this possible. You are the support holding the New England Patriots up. On behalf of the entire organization, I thank you.

As we strive for more championships and even greater heights, we will always reflect on the 2001 season, the events of that year and Super Bowl XXXVI for everything it meant to us. It was more than simply a championship season. It was a lesson in team, fortitude and after September's tragedy, a reminder of the truly important things in our lives.

We will never forget.

Robert Kraft

Robert Kraft

MANAGEMENT, SECOND ROW (L TO R) Vice Chairman Jonathan Kraft, Owner and Chairman Robert Kraft, Head Coach Bill Belichick and Director of Player Personnel Scott Pioli COACHES, SIXTH ROW (L TO R) Brad Seely (special teams), Rob Ryan (outside linebackers), Randy Melvin (defensive line), Eric Mangini (defensive backs), Pepper Johnson (inside linebackers), Brian Daboll (coaching assistant), Romeo Crennel (defensive coordinator), Charlie Weis (offensive coordinator/running backs/quarterbacks), Dante Scarnecchia (assistant head coach/offensive line), Ned Burke (coaching assistant), Jeff Davidson (assistant offensive line), Ivan Fears (wide receivers), Mike Woicik (strength and conditioning) and Markus Paul (assistant strength and conditioning)

STAFF, SEVENTH ROW (L TO R) Frank Mendes (security manager), Ron O'Neil (head trainer), Mike Poirer (intern trainer), Joe Van Allen (assistant trainer), Berj Najarian (executive administrator to head coach), Ernie Adams (football research director), Nick Carparelli (director of operations), Steve Scarnecchia (video assistant), Jimmy Dee (video director), Matt Walsh (video assistant), Fernando Neto (video assistant), John Jastremski (equipment assistant), John Hillebrand (assistant equipment manager), Don Brocher (equipment manager)

2001 PATRIOTS NUMERICAL ROSTER

NO	NAME	POS	EXP	2001 GP/GS/DNP/I	PLAYOFFS GP/GS/DNP/I
4	Adam Vinatieri	PK	6	16/0/0/0	3/0/0/0
11	Drew Bledsoe	QB	9	2/2/7/7	1/0/2/0
12	Tom Brady	QB	2	15/14/1/0	3/3/0/0
13	Ken Walter	P	5	11/0/0/0	3/0/0/0
14	Walter Williams *	RB	R	Injured Reserve	
15	Jimmy Farris	WR	R	0/0/0/0	0/0/0/3
16	Scott McCready *	WR	R	Practice Squad	
19	Damon Huard	QB	5	0/0/7/9	0/0/0/3
21	J.R. Redmond	RB	2	12/0/1/3	3/1/0/0
22	Terrance Shaw	CB	7	13/3/0/3	3/0/0/0
23	Antwan Harris	S	2	11/1/0/5	3/0/0/0
24	Ty Law	CB	7	16/16/0/0	3/3/0/0
25	Leonard Myers	CB	R	7/0/0/9	0/0/0/3
26	Matt Stevens	S	6	15/4/0/1	3/0/0/0
27	Terrell Buckley	CB	10	15/1/0/1	3/0/0/0
28	Brock Williams *	CB	R	Injured Reserve	
29	Hakim Akbar *	S	R	6/0/0/3	Injured Reserve
30	Je'Rod Cherry	S	6	16/0/0/0	3/0/0/0
31	Ben Kelly *	CB	2	2/0/0/4	Injured Reserve
32	Antowain Smith	RB	5	16/15/0/0	3/2/0/0
33	Kevin Faulk	RB	3	15/1/0/1	3/0/0/0
34	Tebucky Jones	FS	4	16/12/0/0	3/3/0/0
35	Patrick Pass	FB	2	16/0/0/0	3/0/0/0
36	Lawyer Milloy	SS	6	16/16/0/0	3/3/0/0
38	Ray Hill *	CB	4	Injured Reserve	
44	Marc Edwards	FB	5	16/13/0/0	3/3/0/0
45	Otis Smith	CB	12	15/15/0/1	3/3/0/0
48	Arther Love	TE	R	0/0/0/6	0/0/0/3
49	Jabari Holloway *	TE	R	Injured Reserve	
50	Mike Vrabel	LB	5	16/12/0/0	3/3/0/0
51	Bryan Cox	LB	11	11/7/0/5	3/0/0/0
52	Ted Johnson	LB	7	12/5/0/4	3/0/0/0
53	Larry Izzo	LB	6	16/0/0/0	3/0/0/0
54	Tedy Bruschi	LB	6	15/9/0/1	3/3/0/0
55	Willie McGinest	DE	8	11/5/0/5	3/1/0/0
58	Matt Chatham	LB	2	11/0/0/3	3/0/0/0
59	Andy Katzenmoyer *	LB	3	Injured Reserve	
60	Drew Inzer *	OL	R	Practice Squad	
61	Stephen Neal	OL	R	0/0/0/3	0/0/0/3
62	Setema Gali *	DE	R	Practice Squad	
63	Joe Andruzzi	G	5	16/16/0/0	3/3/0/0
64	Greg Robinson-Randall	T	2	16/16/0/0	3/3/0/0
65	Damien Woody	C	3	16/15/0/0	3/3/0/0
66	Lonie Paxton	LS	2	16/0/0/0	3/0/0/0
67	Grey Ruegamer	C/G	2	14/1/1/1	3/0/0/0
68	Tom Ashworth *	OL	R	Practice Squad	
70	Adrian Klemm *	T	2	0/0/2/5	Injured Reserve
71	Chris Sullivan	DL	6	0/0/0/3	0/0/0/3
72	Matt Light	T	R	14/12/0/2	3/3/0/0
74	Kenyatta Jones	T	R	5/0/1/10	0/0/0/3
75	Maurice Anderson *	DT	2	Practice Squad	
76	Grant Williams	T	6	14/4/0/2	3/0/0/0
77	Mike Compton	G/C	9	16/16/0/0	3/3/0/0
80	Troy Brown	WR	9	16/13/0/0	3/3/0/0
81	Charles Johnson	WR	8	14/2/0/2	3/0/0/0
82	Curtis Jackson *	WR	2	2/0/1/0	Injured Reserve
83	Rod Rutledge	TE	4	15/14/0/1	3/1/0/0
84	Fred Coleman	WR	1	8/0/0/0	3/0/0/0
85	Jermaine Wiggins	TE	2	16/6/0/0	3/2/0/0
86	David Patten	WR	5	16/14/0/0	3/3/0/0
88	Terry Glenn *	WR	6	4/1/0/8	Suspended
90	Marty Moore*	LB	8	3/0/0/0	Injured Reserve
91	Bobby Hamilton	DE	7	16/15/0/0	3/3/0/0
92	David Nugent	DE	2	9/1/1/1	0/0/0/3
93	Richard Seymour	DT	R	13/10/0/3	3/2/0/0
94	Jace Sayler*	DT	R	2/1/0/1	Injured Reserve
95	Roman Phifer	LB	11	16/16/0/0	3/3/0/0
96	Brandon Mitchell	DT	5	16/11/0/0	3/2/0/0
97	Riddick Parker	DT	5	13/0/1/2	2/1/1/1
98	Anthony Pleasant	DE	12	16/16/0/0	3/3/0/0
99	Kole Ayi *	LB	R	1/0/0/1	Injured Reserve

Players appear numerically from front row to back and left to right across the rows. * Indicates a player not pictured.

CREDITS

JOINTLY PUBLISHED BY | THE NEW ENGLAND PATRIOTS
TEAM POWER PUBLISHING INC.
ÉDITIONS DU TRÉCARRÉ, A DIVISION
OF ÉDITIONS QUEBECOR MÉDIA INC.

PUBLISHER | ALLAN TUROWETZ

AUTHOR | BRYAN MORRY

EDITORS | CHRYS GOYENS, FRED KIRSCH

CREATIVE DIRECTOR | JULIE DESILETS

ART DIRECTOR | BRIGITTE BOUDRIAS

GRAPHIC DESIGNERS | BRIGITTE BOUDRIAS, JULIE DESILETS, FRÉDÉRIC HUARD

PHOTO RESEARCHERS | MARC SEROTA, BRYAN MORRY

PROJECT CO-ORDINATORS | GENEVIÈVE DESROSIERS, MARCIA CURTIS

ACKNOWLEDGMENTS

The following people deserve special recognition for their assistance in making this project possible: Robert and Jonathan Kraft and the entire Kraft family, all of whom kept pro football alive in New England back in 1994; the Patriots coaches and players who brought a championship to New England and gave us reason to create this book; particular thanks goes to Bill Belichick, Romeo Crennel, Charlie Weis and to Berj Najarian for dealing with our constant requests; the staff of *Patriots Football Weekly* and Patriots.com – Paul Perillo, Shane Donaldson, Michelle Muise, Dave Dudek, Carrol Hardy, Trent Adams, Donni Richman, Bob Doyle, Dave Querzoli; the Patriots PR staff – Stacey James, Anthony Moretti, Kathleen Whiteside; the Patriots marketing staff including Lou Imbriano, Jen Ferron and Christine Robillard; Ron Marshall; Joe Mastrangelo; Tom Brady, Sr. and Nancy Brady; Richard Johnson, curator of the Sports Museum of New England; Bill Littlefield, NPR; Bing Broderick, WGBH; Nikki Kirsch and Sarah Morry; the diligent, detail-oriented staff at Team Power Publishing that worked on this project, including Julie Desilets, Brigitte Boudrias, Chrys Goyens, Marc Serota, Geneviève Desrosiers, Marcia Curtis and the Turtle himself, Allan Turowetz.

PHOTO CREDITS

SOURCE PRECEDES PAGE NUMBER, FOLLOWED BY PHOTOGRAPHER'S NAME IN PARENTHESES.

WE HAVE MADE EVERY EFFORT TO TRACE THE OWNERSHIP OF PHOTOS. IF WE HAVE FAILED TO GIVE ADEQUATE CREDIT, WE WILL BE PLEASED TO MAKE CHANGES IN FUTURE PRINTINGS.

NEW ENGLAND PATRIOTS (DAVID SILVERMAN)
4-5, 6, 7, 8-9, 10, 11, 18, 28, 30, 36, 38, 39, 40, 44, 45, 46, 47, 49, 50, 52, 53, 54-55, 56-57, 58, 59, 60, 61, 62, 63, 64, 65, 66, 67, 70, 71, 72, 73, 78-79, 80, 83, 84, 85, 90, 91, 93, 95, 96-97, 98, 101, 102, 105, 106-107, 108, 109, 111, 118, 124, 126, 127, 133, 134, 137, 138, 139, 140, 141, 142, 143, 144, 145, 146, 148, 149, 150-151, 152, 158, 162-163, 164, 168, 172, 173, 174, 176-177, 178, 180, 181, 182, 183, 185, 186, 188, 189, 194, 196, 197, 198-199, 200-201, 202, 203, 204, 206, 207, 208, 209, 210-211, 213, 214, 215, 216-217, 218, 219, 224

NEW ENGLAND PATRIOTS (PETER VENTRONE)
2-3, 10, 11, 45, 46, 47, 48, 91, 92, 93, 94, 95, 98, 99, 104, 108, 109, 111, 112, 113, 114, 115, 116, 122, 123, 125, 127, 130, 133, 137, 138, 152, 153, 154, 156-157, 159, 167, 173, 175, 189, 194, 203, 208, 212, 220-221

NEW ENGLAND PATRIOTS (THOMAS CROKE)
24-25, 28, 30, 32, 34, 35, 100

NEW ENGLAND PATRIOTS (RON DELALLA)
23, 28

NEW ENGLAND PATRIOTS (MARC MASSE)
165, 169

NEW ENGLAND PATRIOTS (ARCHIVES)
10, 14, 16, 17, 19, 20-21, 22, 23, 26, 27, 28, 29, 30, 31, 32, 33, 34, 35, 98, 100, 101, 174

THE BOSTON GLOBE
10, 11, 86, 118, 119, 120-121, 135, 160, 170-171 (MATTHEW LEE); 80, 81, 92, 128-129 (JIM DAVIS); 155 (BARRY CHIN)

ASSOCIATED PRESS
10, 68, 193 (BETH A. KEISER); 75 (DAVID KARP); 76-77 (STAN HONDA); 80, 82 (STEVEN SENNE); 111 (DAVID ZALUBOWSKI); 132 (MIKE GROLL); 136 (BEN MARGOT); 159 (VICTORIA AROCHO); 166 (KEITH SRAKOCIC); 174 (AMY SANCETTA); 180 (DAVE MARTIN); 184, 190-191 (RICK BOWMER); 187 (KATHY WILLENS); 189 (MICHAEL CONROY); 195 (DOUG MILLS)

MARC SEROTA
28, 42-43, 99, 105

NEW YORK TIMES (KELLY GUENTHER)
74, 75

THE BRADY FAMILY
88, 89

WGBH / WHITE MOUNTAIN FILMS
60

ALLSPORT (MATTHEW STOCKMAN)
75

NFL FILMS
92

LAWRENCE EAGLE-TRIBUNE (JUDY EMMERT)
94

PETER THOMAS SNOW
BACK END PAPER

NFL PHOTOS
FRONT END PAPER

INDEX

PAGE NUMBERS IN REGULAR TYPE REFER TO PRINT; PAGE NUMBERS IN ITALICS REFER TO PHOTOS. THE LETTER S BEFORE THE PAGE NUMBER REFER TO SIDEBARS.